presents

Unprecedented Days

90 DAYS OF FIRE

DR. ZACH PROSSER

Prosser

Praying this Book is A Blessing to You

Mt Zion Ridge Press
https://mtzionridgepress.wixsite.com/mtzionridgepress
Copyright © 2018 by Mt Zion Ridge Press

Published in the United States of America
ISBN: 978-1-949564-04-4
Publication Date: December 1, 2018

Editor-In-Chief: Tamera Lynn Kraft, Michelle Levigne
Editor: Jenna Kraft
Cover Artist: Dr. Zach Prosser

Table of Contents

Introduction

Life is full of times and seasons. The plumb line and anchor for every season is the Word of God. It is easy to allow this supernatural hope and life we have been given to lose its passion and joy. God desires to awaken and transform us from one place of glory to the next. Hebrews reminds us to not neglect this great salvation we have been given. This devotional is written from a place of humility to provide an opportunity for God to speak from its pages and bring radical transformation and awakening.

Devotions are combined with Biblical context, understanding of the original texts, and quotes from others who have paved the way for awakening and transformation. Whether challenging or uplifting, the words and insights of these devotions will encourage and edify you in your walk with the Lord. Every day, you can fuel the fire of your passion for God, His Word, and His presence.

Heather and I have spent our lives in passionate pursuit of Christ. Not always have we been perfect, but we find ourselves humbled under the mighty hand of God as He awakens and changes us continually. He is so wonderful and loving and has graciously given us a unique mantle of ministry for revival and awakening.

This devotional has been written in one of those unique seasons of our lives. We love revival and revival history. We believe that the Church has seasons of supernatural awakening and must learn to live in a place of saturation in His presence and His Word. Right now, we have entered one of those fresh seasons in which the Spirit of God is sovereignly awakening and reviving His people. There are those who are not satisfied with religion, who are desperate for God and His transforming power in our generation.

They are repenting and returning to God with their whole heart, and God is healing and reviving the hungry. He truly is faithful to fill those who hunger and thirst for Him.

On July 4, 2018, God's glory came into Celebration Church, the church where we pastor, in an unprecedented way. Lives were resuscitated to their first love of Christ. All the striving after good works began to cease as we entered into the glory of God's rest. Miracles, joy, deliverance, salvation, Baptisms in the Holy Spirit, and signs and wonders have characterized this season. Mostly, we have been amazed by the glory of the God that has come into the room. He always surprises us, and there is never a meeting where we are left wanting. Many times, as His glory comes, a cloud or mist can be seen in the room. We have heard angels singing and angelic music. We have watched as everyone in the room slips to the floor out of awe and humility when His majesty comes in the room. At times the atmosphere seems as though it could explode with great power, as He thunders with glory in the room.

We have witnessed waves of God's joy move through the sanctuary as people are overcome with supernatural joy from another world. Those who are weighed down by life's burdens and tormenting spirits have been liberated. Sickness and disease have been removed. Reports of God's glory touching people and bringing miracles have come from those watching services via the internet.

Now is the time! Let us embrace the work of God in our generation, that this generation may seek Him and experience Him like no other. May this devotion stir the flames of your passion and reignite your first love in Christ. If you have never known this wonderful Savior, Christ Jesus, let today begin the journey of a lifetime.

This gift of salvation is given to you freely today! Simply humble yourself before God, and admit to Him your disobedience. He knows your sin. Are you willing to confess it to Him today? Believe on Christ, the only way to Heaven, and believe that God raised Him from the dead. Confess Him as your Lord and Savior. Tell someone about your decision to follow Christ. Pray right now where you are, and ask Jesus to forgive you and be your Savior. Ask Him to reveal Himself to you and to fill you with His Spirit. If you have done this, the purpose of this devotion book is fulfilled. You are being awakened and transformed one step at a time, and this is the greatest step of your life!

Jesus said to him, "I am the way, the truth, and the life. No one comes to the Father except through Me. (John 14:6, NKJV)

If you confess with your mouth the Lord Jesus and believe in your heart that God has raised Him from the dead, you will be saved. (Romans 10:9, NKJV)

For all have sinned and fall short of the glory of God. (Romans 3:23, NKJV)

For the wages of sin is death, but the gift of God is eternal life in Christ Jesus our Lord. (Romans 6:23, NKJV)

For by grace you have been saved through faith, and that not of yourselves; it is the gift of God, not of works, lest anyone should boast. For we are His workmanship, created in Christ Jesus for good works, which God prepared beforehand that we should walk in them. (Ephesians 2:8-10, NKJV)

Nor is there salvation in any other, for there is no other name under heaven given among men by which we must be saved. (Acts 4:12, NKJV)

For I am not ashamed of the gospel of Christ, for it is the power of God to salvation for everyone who believes. (Romans 1:16a, NKJV)

Endorsement:

Just had the pleasure of reviewing Zach Prosser's book *Unprecedented Days* and I highly recommend it. I have always loved devotionals but find myself gravitating to the old classics like *Morning to Morning* by Charles Spurgeon. Many of the current devotionals seem short on substance. *Unprecedented Days* is quite refreshing and loaded with God's Word and exudes a true sense of revival. This devotional will not only get your day started right, you may just find it ushering you into a new season of revival in your life.

Pastor Frank Bailey
Victory Fellowship, New Orleans

Day One

Just Relax

If God gives such attention to the appearance of wildflowers–most of which are never even seen–don't you think he'll attend to you, take pride in you, do his best for you? What I'm trying to do here is to get you to relax, to not be so preoccupied with getting, so you can respond to God's giving. People who don't know God and the way he works fuss over these things, but you know both God and how he works. Steep your life in God-reality, God-initiative, God-provisions. Don't worry about missing out. You'll find all your everyday human concerns will be met.
Matthew 6:30-33, The Message

Have you ever found yourself in the middle of a stressful situation and wondered how you got there? Even worse, were you worried about how you were going to get out? Maybe there was a time when your young child was stressed out, but as the parent you realized the situation would quickly change and there was no need for the drama.

I love how *The Message Bible* phrases Jesus' words: *What I'm trying to do here is to get you to relax*. We have a saying we use frequently: *Just Drink*. In other words–just chill. Just relax and have a big drink of God's river of living water. Living water will change your stress into joy! Like the parent above, we comfort the child and say, *just relax; it's going to be okay*. After all, stress and anxiety stem from our need to get something. We are stressed about someone not meeting our expectations. We are stressed because we spent more than our income. We are anxious over what the doctor might say. These are all things we are receiving or not receiving that cause stress. We worry about what we are getting.

Why not turn loose of the worry about *getting* and have joy in *giving*? Jesus wants us to stop worrying about our getting and be occupied with God's giving. What is God trying to get into my life? What do I need to turn loose of in order to receive what God is giving? God's giving is *sowing* and *you reap*; *give* and *it will be given*. If you find yourself stressed about the doctor's report, sow joy into someone else. If you find yourself battling loneliness, be a friend to another. Anxious about your finances–give an offering.

A while back I did an illustration with an apple. We know when eating an apple that we do not eat the seeds of the apple. When we cut the apple, we immediately find the seeds and remove them so they are not

5

eaten. Our income is the same. When God gives, we look for the seed. When our *receiving* becomes *a giving*, we move from *worrying* about what we are *getting* to *joy* in *God's giving*.

God has your everyday human concerns handled. This reminds me of someone going into work to do a job they have not been assigned to. It is like someone who is a bookkeeper trying to do the janitor's job. The bookkeeper can be stressed out and anxious about the cobwebs in the building, but they are worried about something outside of their responsibilities. The boss in this organization would remind the bookkeeper that they are concerned about something that they have no control over. We often try to do God's job when we have no control over Him or His responsibilities. He says our job is to *seek first His Kingdom*. The rest is up to Him.

Are you worried and anxious because you want something that God is not giving? Are you driven by a need to get and God is trying to give something greater? Maybe you are anxious about what God is giving, and you would rather hang on to what you already have.

The more you saturate-- or as *The Message* says, *steep*-- your life in God, the more you walk in His reality, His provision, His vision. It is easier to trust Him when your life is full of Him. It is less stressful when God is the central focus and not the fear over what you are getting or not getting in this life. God has clothed the wildflowers of the field in splendor. He will certainly take care of you! Just relax! He's got you covered!

Day Two

Regeneration

Jesus answered and said to him, "Most assuredly, I say to you, unless one is born again, he cannot see the kingdom of God."
John 3:3, NKJV

Regeneration is a word we do not commonly hear these days. It is defined as being reborn or formed again. *Easton's Bible Dictionary* explains *regeneration* as follows:

This word literally means a "new birth." The Greek word so rendered (palingenesia) is used by classical writers with reference to the changes produced by the return of spring. In Matthew 19:28 the word is equivalent to the "restitution of all things" (Acts 3:21). It denotes that change of heart elsewhere spoken of as a passing from death to life; becoming a new creature in Christ Jesus; being born again; a renewal of the mind; a resurrection from the dead; a being quickened. This change is ascribed to the Holy Spirit. It originates not with man but with God. As to the nature of the change, it consists in the implanting of a new principle or disposition in the soul; the impartation of spiritual life to those who are by nature "dead in trespasses and sins." The necessity of such a change is emphatically affirmed in Scripture.

Here in John 3, Jesus describes regeneration as being born again. The instruction to Nicodemus was not something that could be accomplished through his efforts in studying the law or through good works. Nicodemus could not be regenerated by being in a dignified, prestigious religious office. Regeneration occurs only as a work of the Spirit of God.

That which is born of the flesh is flesh, and that which is born of the Spirit is spirit. (John 3:6, NKJV)

This is the life of God at work in the soul of man. As we repent, we are made new. Redemption's effect is this work of regeneration. This is more than turning over a new leaf or endeavoring to be a better you. Regeneration is a complete overhaul of what was. What was once dead is now alive. The sin that was once acceptable is now detestable. The enjoyment of divine things surpasses the hobbies and interests of this life. Those things which are godly and honorable are now delightful and pleasing attributes. The sin that held your conscience captive for so long is erased, and the skeletons in the closet of your mind are removed. The Spirit of God transforms you finally and forever. His work is complete and permanent. Regeneration makes Christ and His work captivating.

Nicodemus was a ruler in the church and should not be associated with Jesus' ministry. Regeneration changed His life and changed His desires. The same man who should not associate with Christ was found burying Him after the crucifixion. He brought 100 pounds of myrrh and aloes to anoint the dead body of Jesus and prepare Him for burial. What changed in Nicodemus? What made him go from a man that sought Christ in the secrecy of the night hour to one who would publicly remove the body of Jesus from the cross and care for the mutilated remains? Regeneration! The words of Jesus echoed clearly that day as Nicodemus anointed that precious body for burial. *Nicodemus, unless a man is born again. Nicodemus, I am the resurrection and the life. As you anoint my body for burial, this body will not remain in the grave. Just as those who come to me, they will be born again. Though they may appear to be dead, I will make them live!*

It is time to allow the anointing of Christ to come upon you that you may live. The regenerating power of God can flow through your life and make you come alive—really alive. Christ is the King who makes all things new. If He can regenerate the lost person, He can certainly quicken you. If you are saddened or discouraged, His anointing power can awaken you. The one who came out of the tomb can bring breakthrough in your life. Like Nicodemus, go to Him at the cross and let the power of Gethsemane's hill flow into you. Run quickly with Nicodemus to the garden tomb where Christ's body was laid, and see the resurrection life that can flow into you. Behold Christ today, and He will bring life into your weary world!

Day Three

Revive Me

Revive me, O Lord, for Your name's sake! For Your righteousness' sake bring my soul out of trouble.
Psalm 143:11, NKJV

Life is filled with trouble. The word used by David for trouble means distress or trouble; sorrow, pain, anguish. David faced the troubles of life. His leader turned on him and tried to kill him. People he trusted left him. His own family tried to defame him. Sin always invites distress. The consequences of sin are sure to find us out–whether by our own sin, the sin of others, or the sin of this world. Sin will always come around and bite us. **The words of the snake may be enticing, but they are filled with venom.** David was not immune and neither are we.

If you have suffered the effects of sin, this verse offers hope: *Revive Me!* David was asking God to sustain his life; to quicken his life in order that he may live. At times the effects of sin may weary you to the point of depression and a desire to no longer live. The effects of sin may take away your strength, your ambition or zeal. But in the midst of his agony, David cried to the Lord for life! This is supernatural life. It is the God-kind of life given by the work of His presence. It's the life of God in the soul man. Romans 8:11 tells us that the same Spirit that raised Christ from the dead will quicken us.

Is the Spirit of God living in you? Have you become the temple of the Holy Spirit? If He has taken up residence within you, you have the same person that brought the crucified Christ out of His grave. The same Spirit that quickened Lazarus is in you. The same Spirit that raised the widow's son is in you. The same Spirit that raised the Shunammite's son is living in you. And if He is in you, He can revive you to new life.

God will work this miracle in you based not on your merit, but according to His name. David said, "for your name's sake!" Translated from Hebrew, David is saying, "according to or for the purpose of your reputation or glory" quicken or revive me. It is the desire of God to revive you, not by the works of your own righteousness that is like dirty laundry, but according to His righteousness and fame which is perfect and holy. His motive in reviving you is pure, without manipulation. He is not demanding a hidden agreement; there is no fine print to read. God desires that you be revived according to his righteousness for His own glory.

What a divine picture! God desires you to be quickened and full of life that His glory might be put on display for others to see. You are a living epistle. You are God's masterpiece. He has displayed you for the world to see His work in you. You are incapable of reviving yourself. No person when they are dying are able to administer resuscitation on themselves. We must have the hand of God massage our heart to life and breathe life into our nostrils.

Lord, revive me! I do not know what others may decide. I do not know how others may respond to my new life. All I know is that I am dying without you. For your glory and my enjoyment, will you come? The same Spirit that regenerated me at salvation can renew the joy of my salvation. The same Spirit that made me alive to Christ can sustain and quicken this divine life I am living. Have the troubles of life got you down? Christ can raise you up and quicken you to new life!

Day Four

Night of Hope

But at midnight Paul and Silas were praying and singing hymns to God...
Acts 16:25, NKJV

Can you imagine being beaten and imprisoned for no crime other than being used of God to set a demon possessed person free? Paul and Silas were completely innocent of a crime, and guilty only of loving the hurting and the broken.

Our church has an outreach called *Night of Hope*. It was launched as we were asking God to give us a vision to reach our community in a unique way. Much like Paul and Silas, this ministry often comes to people at their darkest hour. We have the privilege of loving those who feel as though they are in bondage or are broken by life's hang ups and hurts.

We have given away groceries, hot meals, haircuts, spa treatments, medical screenings, chiropractic adjustments, vaccinations, resources, and community assistance. Beyond the tangible ministry, the Gospel has been preached and demonstrated. We have walked with families through death, drug addiction, financial hardship, and salvation.

What had become the midnight hour for Paul and Silas came as the result of bringing the radiance of the Son into a darkened life. Here was a woman bound to her masters and bound to a demon. The fortune telling woman encountered God. In one moment, the brightness of God's glory invaded her life and liberated her from bondage. It was that miracle that brought Paul and Silas to the prison. But at midnight — in their darkness — they were able to sing out songs of praise because they trusted in God. **They had seen His power liberate the demoniac, and they knew that His same power could liberate them from their prison walls.**

Are you afflicted today in bondage and brokenness? Has hardship overcome you in this life? Have you seen the spiritual condition in which you lie helpless? The light of God's glory can liberate you from all oppression! Are you a friend of God discouraged by circumstance? Have you come into a dark place because of your good works? Do you, like Lazarus, feel you have given all for your friend Jesus, and yet He has allowed you to die? Be encouraged! Jesus is on His way to your tomb. Be edified! The resurrection life that liberated the demoniac has come to liberate you.

You can look at your night and say this is a place of hope. Others may have prospered from this woman's fortune telling, but what had been sown in darkness would now be reaped in everlasting life. God took her out of her night and brought her into His marvelous light that she might proclaim His wonderful works. God delivered Paul and Silas out of their night and into the light of His joy.

God brought hope to Paul and Silas, and He brought hope to the prison jailer. God used a night of beating, torment, and imprisonment to bring salvation to the jailer and his family. In just a matter of hours, they witnessed the power of God set the demoniac free, save the jailer, and save the jailer's family. God delivered the tormented, the tortured, and the trembling persons. He brought hope in the midst of hardship. He will do the same for you!

Day Five

One Desire Above All

One thing I have desired of the Lord, that will I seek: That I may dwell in the house of the Lord all the days of my life, to behold the beauty of the Lord.
Psalm 27:4, NKJV

Our lives have the tendency to be filled with so many things: family, relationships, career, finances, health. We can often spend hours talking about the things happening in our lives.

Here we find David declaring out his single focus and single passion — God I need you more than anything. Not that David was always perfect in His focus, but when he was distracted, he was quick to repent and return to this one desire.

We are all born with desire. Babies from birth want to be held and nurtured by their mother and cry for this affection. Babies communicate their desire for food when they are hungry. Desire still motivates us to action as we get older. We see and experience things in life that are pleasing and pleasurable and thus desires are formed.

How are spiritual desires formed and fed? David answers this in Psalms 27 also. The fulfillment of the desire of His heart also feeds the desire from which it springs forth: *I may dwell in the house of the Lord all the days of my life, to behold the beauty of the Lord.* Observing God in His house and gazing upon His beauty ignites a desire for more of Him.

You can observe God in His house by enjoying His presence in your private times of prayer and worship. Seeing and savoring His sweetness happens as you see Him move among your spiritual family in church or small groups. Delighting in God can be done as you see Him revealed in Scripture. Observe Him in His splendor in the avenues by which He reveals Himself and you will desire to see Him more.

Gazing upon the beauty of the Lord will leave you in awe and wonder. Like Jeremiah, you will say, *There is none like you, O LORD; you are great, and your name is great in might* (Jeremiah 10:6, ESV).

Have you been awakened to the Lord's beauty? Like David, is your heart beating with a single desire to know Him passionately and intimately? If not, let this be your goal before God: to observe Him in His sanctuary. Ask Him to reveal Himself to you. Like Moses, be bold enough to ask God to show you His glory. God never disappoints, and one moment of revelation will change your life—it will change your desires. Like David, be quick to repent and return to your first love.

As you see Him, allow desire for Him to rise and continue. Do not be like the foolish virgins that are lulled to sleep when the Master is calling. The world and your carnal nature will tell you that desiring God is emotionalism, irrational, or radical. The writers of the Bible will tell you another story. The Holy Spirit will reveal something greater. Allow your passion for God to grow, and deepen your desire for more of Him!

Day Six

For Such a Time

Yet who knows whether you have come to the kingdom for such a time as this?
Esther 4:14, NKJV

How wonderful is the call of God on our lives! He brings us out of our orphaned state, adopts us as His children, and makes us His instruments of praise. Esther's story is a great example of the life-transforming work of God. She became the instrument of praise to declare the salvation of God for her people.

Have you considered the work of God in you lately? He has awakened you to His love. He has immersed you into His presence. He has purified you and washed the stench of sin from you. God has anointed you with His fragrant oils and placed within your mouth a new song of joy. He has brought you to the Kingdom for such a time as this! Alexander MacLaren expounds on this verse from Esther here:

Who knoweth whether thou art come to the kingdom for such a time as this? There speaks the devout statesman, the court-experienced believer. He has seen favourites tended and tossed aside, viziers powerful and beheaded, kings half deified and deserted in their utmost need. Sitting at the gate there, he has seen generations of Hamans go out and in; he has seen the craft, the cruelty, the lusts which have been the apparent causes of the puppets' rise and fall, and he has looked beyond it all and believed in a Hand that pulled the wires, in a King of Kings who raiseth up one and setteth down another. So he believes that his Esther has come to the kingdom by God's appointment, to do God's work at God's time. And these convictions keep him calm and stir her.

No man receives the Gospel for his own sake. We are not non-conductors, but stand all linked hand in hand. We are members of the body that the blood may flow freely through us. For no loftier reason did God light the candle than that it might give light. We are beacons kindled to transmit, till every sister light flashes back the ray.

Now is the time for you to arise and radiate the glory of the Lord. His message is redemption, and His plan is salvation. He is baptizing people in the Holy Spirit. He is breaking bondages and cleansing the captives. God has positioned you, given you power, and filled your mouth with praise. Now is the time to release the sound. Now is the time to minister to the broken. Now is the time to freely give as you have freely received.

Do you lack assurance in His assignment? Do you lack confidence in His commission? Have you felt that you are incapable to minister to the broken? What timidity keeps you from speaking to the hurting? Be reminded of how God has orchestrated your steps, redeemed you from the pit, washed you from faithlessness, and immersed you in the boldness of His Spirit. Let your light shine so that all men might see your Father's radiance. You have come to the Kingdom, and now you have been made an ambassador of the King.

Day Seven

I'm in Need of Him Alone

My soul thirsts for God, for the living God...
Psalm 42:2, NKJV

In his book *The Real Faith,* Charles Price tells the story of a crippled man who was continually brought into the services for healing. Price and others spent much time praying for the man. Days went by and there was no sign of healing.

One afternoon they wheeled him to a corner in the building. He asked the people to leave the two of us alone, and then said something that has lingered in the chambers of my memory. "What a failure I am," he declared. "I came here strong in what I thought was my faith in the Lord. As I look deeply into my heart I find something about which I wish to confess. What a poor, miserable failure I have been. I have been spiritually proud of the fact that people have pointed to me as a man who suffered without complaining. They pointed me out as the man who never grumbled, although he had a cross to bear. I grew proud of my reputation and I can see now that what I termed my goodness has been self-righteousness in the sight of my Lord."

"Dr. Price," he said, "I don't need healing half as much as I need Jesus. I am so hungry for His presence. More than anything else in my life, I want to know Him better, and I am content to spend my days in this chair if only He will flood this self-righteous heart of mine with His peace and love."

Dr. Price describes how he watched the crippled man in the wheelchair disappear around the corner of the building after that conversation. A few days later, this man came back to the church for the evening service. He described to Dr. Price how Jesus had met him the night before. He spent the night in prayer and praise and worship. He described how the fog had lifted from his heart and mind, and he became conscious of an infusion of Life Divine.

"Why does this man have to wait until tonight?" "He does not," I replied. "The Great Physician is here now. Jesus of Nazareth is passing by." A moment later it was over. Out of his wheelchair arose that man. He ran and jumped and praised the Lord for his deliverance.

Our God is the Great Physician, and He desires to heal. Just as much as He is our healer, He is our creator. If you were to be admitted to

Heaven's triage, the first condition of healing to apply would be that of your heart. What offense or spiritual pride lingers there? The cancer of your heart must be cleansed for the life of God to flow into every spiritual extremity. Jesus wants to heal every brokenness, and it is of great importance that your inner man be made whole.

Do you desire to be healed only in the external, or is there a desperation for utter deliverance–spirit, soul and body? Let the sickness of vanity and pride be cleansed and love-sickness for your first love return. Let your inner man be restored from its blockages that it may be moved with compassion for the lost. Cleanse your soul from every hindrance that the rivers of life may flow freely from within. The Healer is able to heal your physical body, but He also has great concern for your spirit man and soul. May the cry of your heart be: *I don't need healing half as much as I need Jesus. I am so hungry for His presence.*

Day Eight

It's Easy to Receive

Assuredly, I say to you, unless you are converted and become as little children, you will by no means enter the kingdom of heaven.
Matthew 18:3, NKJV

What is it that you need from the Lord? Is it direction for your path? Do you need divine healing, divine providence, divine wisdom? Where you lack, He can supply. There is a bountiful, surpassing overflow of perfect gifts available to you in Christ.

Every good gift and every perfect gift is from above, coming down from the Father of lights, with whom there is no variation or shadow due to change (James 1:17, ESV).

We can come to our Father knowing He will not give us a stone instead of bread (Matt 7:9). He has gracious and wonderful gifts to bestow upon His children who will come to Him in faith. He is the Reward and Rewarder of those who diligently seek Him in faith (Heb 11:6). Our Heavenly Father is neither changed by circumstance or diminished by need. With Him there is no variation or shadow due to change. He is always at His zenith. The brightness of His glory is always brightly radiant and continually flowing forth like a perpetual spring of water that neither ends nor is quenched.

Have you become as a humble child with the persuasion of your Father's love? It might be that there are times we do not receive because we withhold ourselves in timidity instead of coming before the Father like a child, confident of His love. Does sickness linger in your body because, while you understand Him to be a loving Father, you have yet to come to Him in faithful assurance. Receive of the Father's love which is continually pouring out in crashing tides that might catch you away like an ocean's billowing waves.

Healing is not dependent upon the development of a perfect faith by any process of self, but rather contact with Jesus (Charles Price).

You may humble yourself before Him and request the faith to embrace Him. Like the woman with the issue of blood who had heard of Christ's power, you may come trembling and unclean into the crowd, and leave completely whole as you make contact with Him through faith. He is willing that you come to Him, and He desires that you come to Him. It is through simple childlike faith that you obtain Him and the precious promises He has made available to you. It requires no striving or power of the mind to obtain. The promises of His blessing are not spells that can be chanted until some magic occurs. His Word concerning you is His promise—His declaration concerning you. If He has spoken of healing in His Word for you, then healing can be received. If He has spoken of salvation in His Word for you, then salvation can be received. Ask the author of His Word to reveal His promise concerning you, and may the Revealer of this Word impart the faith to obtain all that He has spoken.

With childlike humility we may receive the faith which receives the Reward and the Rewarder. Like the child in Matthew 18, Christ is positioning you in the place to receive all He has spoken. Today is your day to receive!

Day Nine

Vulnerability

And they continued steadfastly in the apostles' doctrine and fellowship...
Acts 2:42, NKJV

Webster describes the origin of the word *vulnerable* as originating from
the Latin noun *vulnus* or *wound*. *Vulnus* led to the Latin verb *vulnerare*,
meaning *to wound,* and then to the Late Latin adjective *vulnerabilis,* which
became *vulnerable* in English in the early 1600's. *Vulnerable* originally
meant *capable of being physically wounded* or *having the power to wound* (the
latter is now obsolete), but since the late 1600's, it has also been used
figuratively to suggest a defenselessness against non-physical attacks. In
other words, someone (or something) can be vulnerable to criticism or
failure as well as to literal wounding.

The word denotes a sense of letting down one's defenses — becoming
open and receptive. Vulnerability is a key in community. To have true
fellowship requires those in the community to let down their guard and
become transparent. Figuratively, it is not merely allowing others to look
at your yard through the privacy fence; it is actually removing the fence
altogether and allowing others into your space.

The Bible uses a Greek word *Koinonia* to help paint this picture. It means
fellowship, intimacy, joint participation, or camaraderie. It is the sharing
of mutual risk and mutual benefit. In Christ's community, this is
expressed in the joining of many backgrounds, diversities, and
experiences into one Body with Christ as the head.

I used to run a communal living discipleship home for men. In this sense
of community, everyone shared not only space and housing, but our
lives. If someone in the house was having a bad day, everyone noticed. If
there was a success, we all rejoiced. Challenges were faced collectively,
not just individually. This environment demanded vulnerability.

Our community in Christ demands vulnerability. When God is
convicting and challenging you, community requires vulnerability to
share this conviction with others. As James says: *confess your faults to one
another and pray for one another that you may be healed* (James 5:16).
Community requires outdoing one another with love and honor
(Romans 12:10). This means you are intentionally looking for ways to

bless one another. Vulnerability means that you walk in forgiveness with your community before you offer your worship (Matt 18). There are nearly 60 commands in Scripture that begin with "one another." Vulnerability requires walking in community with others.

Ask God to help you let down the walls of fear and pride and become vulnerable within your community. There is no command in scripture that you must score 100% on an entrance exam for Christ's community. Consider those who followed Jesus: drunks, murderers, thieves, prostitutes, business people, religious people. Come as you are into His community. Let down the walls with your fellow brothers and sisters in Christ. See what power flows in community as it did in the New Testament church.

The words in this verse *"continued steadfastly"* means *to be preserved in; kept from spoiling; or maintain for future use.* There is a direct link between your involvement in Christ's community and your spiritual preservation. The moment you disconnect from divine fellowship within the Body of Christ, you begin to spoil. At this point some may offer excuses such as offense, hurt, wrongful actions by church leadership, and the like. While unfortunate things happen within the Church, the Church is God's plan for your spiritual life and fellowship. Walking through these difficulties perfects you and shapes you as you humble yourself before God.

Today is a new day to walk in community with vulnerability. Take the small step of opening up to someone about what God is doing in your life. Share a Scripture that has been meaningful to you. Pray for one another. Look for way to bless others. You might be surprised at the power of God that flows into your life through community!

Day Ten

Faith of a Seed for Healing

So the Lord said, "If you have faith as a mustard seed, you can say to this mulberry tree, 'Be pulled up by the roots and be planted in the sea,' and it would obey you."
Luke 17:6, NKJV

To believe in healing is one thing, but to have faith for it is something completely different. To trust that God is able to heal is one thing, but to know Him as your Healer is entirely another. Faith is applicable for more than healing—the very essence of our salvation is founded in faith. For the moment, however, let me specifically address faith for healing.

Consider the faith that was needed for your salvation. Did you create this faith? Were you redeemed from the awful pits of hell because you gave mental credence to a doctrine? Faith was imparted to you through the reality of Christ's gift by the Holy Spirit. The Holy Spirit enables us to hear what the natural ear cannot. This is why Jesus spoke of religious leaders having ears but they could not hear. The message of Christ was being proclaimed, and the ministry of Christ was being demonstrated — yet they were still darkened to His reality. It is an awful thing to be face to face with His presence and still be unaware He is even in the room.

Remember that faith, even the weight of a single mustard seed, can do more than a ton of determination or wishful thinking. True faith, when it is present, produces results just as the sun when it has risen produces light. It is inevitable that faith brings God-results. When needing a healing from the Lord, so many people come to the Lord on the basis of His Word. They *try and try* to affirm they are healed by repetition or having some mindset of healing. Herein lies a fundamental problem. Faith is not repetition of words nor a mental state. We have made difficult what God intends to be easy.

Galatians 5:22 tells us that faith is a fruit of the Spirit. Who is responsible for this work of faith in our lives? The Holy Spirit! When New Testament saints were faced with persecution, was it the natural man's tendency to love the unlovely? Of course not. It was God's love shed abroad in their heart according to Romans 5:5. It was the wonderful fruit of love from God. Belief is an element of faith, but the fruit of faith is more than belief. It is a fruit that is produced as we are connected to the vine.
Instead of operating in condemnation over lack of faith or being anxious

about faith, why not ask the giver of faith to impart this wonderful fruit into your life? It does not take much. Even an amount much smaller than the size of the smallest blueberry can remove mountains. Faith is the assurance, conviction, and certainty of God's promise. Faith is being fully persuaded by God of God's promise and His work. Faith cannot be produced by people. Faith is God's warranty certifying the revelation He has birthed in you will come to pass in His way and His time. Faith in God's Word is the guarantee from God, planted in us, that everything He has spoken in His Word will come to pass. I am not confused about my salvation because I have faith from God, in God, and by God that I am born again. Faith for healing operates the same in that it is from God, in God, and by God you are healed and restored. Today, ask God for faith regarding your healing.

Day Eleven

Don't Profane the Holy

By those who come near Me I must be regarded as holy; and before all the people I must be glorified.
Leviticus 10:3, NKJV

The story of Nadab and Abihu is a shocking encounter with God. It reminds me of the New Testament account of Ananias and Sapphira. In both occurrences, the individuals involved were profaning the holiness of God.

The New King James uses the word "profane" to describe Nadab and Abihu's fire. Some translations call it "strange." The Hebrew says it is *estranged, foreign, loathsome, that of a prostitute.* The description here is that Nadab and Abihu were performing what was to be holy worship in the wrong manner—a manner that was offensive to a holy God. What is dedicated to the Lord can neither be taken for personal gain or attributed to another. They took the presence of the Lord as commonplace, and the fire of the altar consumed them. They decided to act according to their own judgment and did not follow the pattern God had given them for worship.

What was God's pattern? God had already given direction to Moses and Aaron that He is to be regarded as holy and must be glorified. If we are to honor God, we must do as God commanded ; we recognize there is none like Him, we recognize His heavy or weighty presence, and we exalt Him. This was more than understanding a dogma of God's holiness. Those present that day witnessed the reality of God's glory for themselves. God is looking for worshippers who worship more than concept. He is looking for pure worship that is in order with His holiness. Watching the fire from the altar leap out and burn these two men to death left an unforgettable memory in the minds of those who saw the reality of God's holiness. Watching Ananias and Sapphira fall to their feet dead left a lasting impression of God's holiness upon those who witnessed this account. Let us never forget the holiness of God, and may we never lack in awe and reverence for Him.

Alexander MacLaren continues this thought about Nadab and Abihu:

They have had many successors, not only in Israel, while a ritual demanding punctilious conformity lasted, but in Christendom since. Alas! our censers are often flaming with 'strange fire.' How much so-called Christian worship glows with self-will or with partisan zeal! When we seek to worship God for what we can get, when we rush into His presence with hot, eager desires which we have not subordinated to His will, we are burning 'strange fire which He has not commanded.' The only fire which should kindle the incense in our censers, and send it up to heaven in fragrant wreaths, is fire caught from the altar of sacrifice. God must kindle the flame in our hearts if we are to render these else cold hearts to Him.

Let your life be consecrated to worship the Lord in Spirit and Truth. He calls us today to come boldly into His presence based on Christ's sacrifice. Efforts to come into God's holy presence based on any other work will find us in the company of Nadab, Abihu, Ananias, and Saphira. Literal fire may not come from the altar and consume you, but it will be impossible to delight in God's presence with dishonor towards Him in your heart.

Day Twelve

Don't Trust the Snake

The God of peace will soon crush Satan under your feet.
Romans 16:20, NASB

Have you ever felt like every time you turn around the enemy was out to stop you from advancing–relationship issues, financial trouble, doubt in God's Word? Our God is a God of peace. The word here used for "peace" means "to be in a place of rest or tranquility; free from rage or war." The word for "soon" means "with haste or speed." Our God of tranquility and victory will quickly crush the enemy under YOUR feet!

Here, the word for "crushed" means to "smash, utterly destroy, break into pieces, obliterate, demolish." Your victory is guaranteed because Christ is demolishing the power of the enemy from your life. In Christ, every chain is pulverized. In Christ, every bondage is utterly destroyed. In Christ, every distraction is laid to waste. In Christ, every lie is broken into pieces.

Christ has made you victorious over every temptation, every sin, and even death itself. Furthermore, He is working out in you this victory through every step you take on His path. Christ paid for your ultimate freedom, and we learn to live out this freedom, crushing the enemy as we walk out our divine purpose in Christ! Every step is a blow to the enemy. Every act of worship is crushing and grinding the old venomous head.

Andrew MacClaren expounds on this verse:

Yes, it is God that bruises, but He uses our feet to do it. It is God from whom the power comes, but the power works through us, and we are neither merely the field, nor merely the prize, of the conflict between these two, but we ourselves have to put all our pith into the task of keeping down the flat, speckled head that has the poison gland in it. 'The God of peace'-blessed be His Name-'shall bruise Satan under your feet,' but it will need the tension of your muscles, and the downward force of your heel, if the wriggling reptile is to be kept under.

Determine today to walk in victory. In Christ, walk according to the path of peace. This does not mean distractions and attacks will not come. It means that you are determined to lay a defeating blow by the power of God by each step you take with Christ. It means you continue worshipping. It means you continue praying. It means you continue walking in your God-given authority. You will not be bitten by the venom of bitterness or offense.

Paul is encouraging the believers to not succumb to the harassment of those trying to cause division in the church. Likewise, believers are to set their focus on the God of peace and not allow the attacks of others trying to cause them to stumble. When our eyes are fastened on Him and our delight is in Him, it is more difficult to be ensnared by temptation or poisoned by venom.

Lift your shout of praise. Exalt the Lord and make your boast in Him. The God of peace has brought to you victory over every scheme of the doomed reptile the Devil! There is no obstacle in your path that God has not defeated and nothing He cannot guide you through!

Day Thirteen

Kingdom of Joy

For the kingdom of God is not a matter of eating and drinking but of
righteousness and peace and joy in the Holy Spirit.
Romans 14:17, ESV

People continually are trying to find fulfillment and pleasure. Some work hard in their careers to find a sense of fulfillment and delight. Others pursue hobbies and entertainment. Still others indulge in worldly, sinful activities. Yet, how many say, "I will find my fulfillment and my pleasure in God and His church?" Is this at the top of the career-minded person's list of pleasure? Is finding delight in God on the top of the thrill seeker's bucket list? Even the religious–do they have a longing for absolute satisfaction in God, or are they seeking a sense of identity by the dogma they know and the religious checkboxes marked on their rites and ritual list?

Here, Paul teaches us plainly that we should cease our striving and enter into the Kingdom way of righteousness, peace, and joy in the Holy Spirit. Thrills and delights at the ballgame are considered to be normal. Getting excited, showing emotion, and having a good time in any area of life other than church seems to be approved by others. But to tell someone they can have more delight and joy in the Holy Spirit elicits strange looks and religious vomit. Laughter and dancing in the presence of the Lord is frowned upon. Why would a joyful God expect those He loves to find greater joy outside of Him? Seems that this would break the first and greatest commandment to love God first. If we love Him more than any other, our greatest delight is in Him more than any other.

Joy in God is more than finding some sense of self awareness in meditation. Joy in God is more than feeling accomplished by attending a church service or special religious event. Joy in God is more than even finding a temporary happiness from a good sermon. Joy in God is pure and the zenith of all joys. It brings delight, laughter, enjoyment, liberty, peace, dancing, shouting, clapping, lifting of hands, singing of songs, declaring His greatness, and much more. Heaven is not a quiet place–but is filled with the sounds of joy and delight in God.

Today, you can delight in God more than any other–more than entertainment, more than a good movie, more than another concert, more than a good book, more than a party, more than another drink, more than another relationship, more than another career. Delight in God will leave you changed! If you have a view that heaven, delight in God, and religion are nothing more than fat cherubs sitting on clouds playing harps while the saints sit in white robes telling "war stories" from their life on earth, you have missed Biblical Christianity. It's time to delight in God!

God is the highest good of the reasonable creature. The enjoyment of Him is our [sic] *proper; and is the only happiness with which our souls can be satisfied. To go to heaven, fully to enjoy God, is infinitely better than the most pleasant accommodations here. Better than fathers and mothers, husbands, wives, or children, or the company of any, or all earthly friends. These are but shadows; but the enjoyment of God is the substance. These are but scattered beams; but God is the sun. These are but streams; but God is the fountain. These are but drops, but God is the ocean.* (Jonathan Edwards)

Today, it's time to jump into the ocean of His joy! No longer do you need to attempt pleasure at "drops in the bucket," but dive into the ocean of His fullness. You will not be disappointed!

Day Fourteen

Streams in Dry Places

He will be like a hiding place from the wind, a shelter from the storm, like streams of water in a dry place, like the shade of a great rock in a weary land.
Isaiah 32:2, ESV

Have you ever been dehydrated? Your whole body is affected by dehydration. Common symptoms might include dry mouth, headache, dry skin, muscle cramps, and lack of energy. Extreme dehydration leads to death. Spiritual dehydration can be just as serious and look very similar. Someone lost in the spiritual barren places, cut off from the source of water, can begin to have "mouth" problems or problems with the things they speak. Spiritual dehydration can lead to confusion and lack of clarity. This ailment can cause one to be rough and harsh or unloving. Any use of spiritual exercise or limbs can cause cramps and discomfort. Eventually, spiritual dehydration can lead to burnout, lack of zeal, and death. Unfortunately, dehydration affects the entire body, and not just one member.

Isaiah is prophesying concerning Christ. He will reign as a righteous King. He describes Christ as a rock in weary places, a shelter in the midst of the desert storm, and streams of water in the barren land. Jesus spoke of himself in John 7 as the one who would give limitless divine water to drink. This spiritual drink would become, in its partakers, a river of living water flowing from within. Those who are thirsty can come and drink freely without reservation.

Jonathan Edwards describes Christ as this river of living water this way:

He shall be as "rivers of water in a dry place." This is an allusion to the deserts of Arabia, which was an exceedingly hot and dry country. One may travel there many days, and see no sign of a river, brook, or spring, nothing but a dry and parched wilderness; so that travelers are ready to be consumed with thirst, as the children of Israel were when they were in this wilderness, when they were faint because there was no water. Now when a man finds Jesus Christ, he is like one that has been traveling in those deserts 'til he is almost consumed with thirst, and who at last finds a river of cool and clear water. And Christ was typified by the river of water that issued out of the rock for the children of Israel in this desert: he is compared to a river, because there is such a plenty and fullness in him.

31

Drinking of the river of God is not a one-time taste any more than drinking of natural water is not a one-time experience. Though one drink of God's river is enough to save and transform, no one who has truly tasted of its delight can only have one enjoyment. Throughout Scripture we are encouraged to keep drinking–keep receiving–from God's sustaining power. Jesus told us to remain in Him. Drinking of the river of God is learning to live in the waters of life, not drinking and return to life as usual. After all, who can return to normal life after drinking of such divine water!

Day Fifteen

Get Your House in Order

Pass through the camp and command the people, saying, "Prepare provisions for yourselves, for within three days you will cross over this Jordan, to go in to possess the land which the LORD your God is giving you to possess."
Joshua 1:11, NKJV

The Lord has called you to possess the promised land. Maybe the land that it is time to possess is the salvation of your family. It could be time to see your neighborhood affected by the presence of the Lord. God could be speaking to you about a new ministry or small group. Where have you settled for anything less than possessing your promise? What land is God calling you into?

Moses had died and the Israelites were in mourning. It took boldness in the Lord to step out and face the fears of what is to come. It took faith to walk into this promise differently than they had walked into the promise in the past. Moses was no longer holding a rod over the river's waters; the priests had to step out with the ark of God's presence before the waters would roll back. There was uncertainty as to who or what would be awaiting them on the other side.

Your first step in possessing your promise is preparing your provision. Joshua gave word to prepare yourself. In other words, get yourself, your family, and your belongings in order. What in your home and your family needs to be brought into order so that you can step fully into your promise? I would imagine some of the people had to leave things behind. Others had to have some family conversations about what was to happen. People had to leave their mourning over what was and step into what God was doing today. There were others who may have had to deal with conflicts that they had with Joshua and his leadership. God had placed His hand on Joshua to lead the way. Before you can possess your promise, God will bring order to your home, your family, and your possessions.

If your financial stewardship is not Biblically aligned, you will miss the promise. If your family altar is not aligned, you are in danger of missing the promise. A family altar, a place of prayer and devotion within your family is imperative to walking in the promises of God together. Perhaps there is someone like Lot's wife hanging out in your family–someone who is not moving in the direction the Lord is calling. You will find

33

yourself being hindered in receiving the promise. God will begin to bring order in your family and your home so that you may cross over into your promise land.

Perhaps the first step for you is to "prepare" your home. This word prepare in the Hebrew is to establish, fix or make firm, or set in order. Here's how God is "preparing" you:

Establish: To make permanent or to get the facts in order
Psalm 1 – He's planting you with roots in His Word so that you will not falter when walking into your promise.

Make Firm: Resolute and determined
Hebrews 10:23 – *You will not waver, but walk in faith.*

Set in Order: Authoritative Direction or Organization
James 4:7 – *Submit to God.* Submit to His Authority. YIELD! To be fully yielded to God leaves no room to entertain the devil.

Day Sixteen

Draw Me Away

Draw me away! We will run after you.
Song of Solomon 1:4, NKJV

Solomon begins this chapter with the Shulamite longing for the kisses of her lover. What a picture of our desire for Christ. *Let Him kiss me with the kisses of his mouth–for your love is better than wine.* (SOS 1:2). He continues this passion and desire for love into verse 4: *Draw me away!*

He wants to captivate His children. The Lord wants our full attention and desires. The Lord wants us to hear His call to run after Him. What would distract you from His affection today? What sin or weight would hold you back from running after Him? The Lord wants to bring you closer–bring you into His chamber of love.

Life and its issues can distract us. Our eyes get fixed on our problems. Our heart gets wounded by the unmet expectations of others. We become offended and burdened down with weights. We ask ourselves if we can ever find rest and happiness in God. Is it really possible? All we see is the baggage. All we feel is the hurt and anxiety. But today, Jesus is calling after you. He wants to draw you away. He wants the burdens to melt away and for you to run after Him.

He is awakening your passion for Him. He is awakening your desire for Him. He is calling out to you on your bed. He is calling out to you in His creation. He is calling out to you through your family or your coworker. He is beckoning for you to run after Him. The Spirit of God is wooing you and captivating your attention towards Christ.

Here is how Jonathan Edwards describes this captivation:

The more sensitive a conscience is in a diseased soul, the less easily it is quieted without a real healing. The influence of the Spirit of God is even more clearly demonstrated when people have their hearts drawn away from the world. The Spirit weans them from the objects of their worldly lusts and takes from them worldly pursuits. He accomplishes this by giving them the sense of excellency of divine things and affection for spiritual enjoyments of another world that are promised in the Gospel.

Can you see the enjoyments of another world? Can you hear the sounds and taste the delights of heaven? Has the Word of God and its enjoyments become real to you? Jesus is calling out to you. Will you run after Him?

In our pursuit of God, all the distractions fall away. We are enticed by Him, pleasured by Him, and desire only Him. This is our first love. This is our passion. He longs to awaken in His bride a deeper passion, a deeper sense of His love, and a deeper longing to be like Him and with Him.

Lord, draw us away! Captivate our attention away from this world and its lusts. Pull us into you a little closer. May we not resist your tender mercies today.

Day Seventeen

The Mercy and Wrath of God

Kiss the Son, lest He be angry, and you perish in the way, when His wrath is kindled but a little. Blessed are all those who put their trust in Him.
Psalm 2:12, NKJV

Consider today the great mercies of God that have been poured out upon you. It is because the Creator has stepped into His creation and bestowed lavishly His grace and His mercy that we are not consumed. Lamentations tells us that it is because of the Lord's mercies that we are not consumed. His lovingkindness towards us is new every morning.

The scepter of God's mercy has been extended to you in the cross. The blood of forgiveness has been applied to the mercy seat. Access into the holy place–the very presence of God has been given. Come today and find mercy for your life.

The grace of God will transform your life. Kiss the Son and find that nearness to His heart will compel you deeper into His love. Kiss the Son and hear His heartbeat as it beats in compassion for you. Kiss the Son and feel the breath of His Spirit upon your cheek. Kiss the Son and know that place of intimacy and change for yourself.

As there is great mercy at the throne of God for you, there is also great wrath towards those who do not come with a kiss of humility. Like Mary who anointed the feet of Jesus, you can kiss the Son in worship, or like Judas you can kiss the Son in betrayal. Judas kissed the Son unto judgement, but we are invited to kiss the Son in His mercy. Judas betrayed the One who came with mercy and forgiveness. His kiss of betrayal brought guilt and judgment.

Oh, the fierceness of the wrath of God that is upon those who do not kiss the Son in worship. Jonathan Edwards had quite the ability to describe this wrath of God:

The wrath of God is like great waters that are damned for the present. They increase more and more and rise higher and higher, till an outlet is given. The higher the stream is stopped, the more rapid and mighty is its course when it is let loose. If God should only withdraw His hand from the floodgate, it would immediately fly open, and the fiery floods of the fierceness and wrath of God would rush forth with inconceivable fury. They would come upon you with omnipotent power. Even if your strength were ten thousand times greater that it is–even ten thousand times greater than the strength of the stoutest devil in hell–it would be nothing to withstand or endure it.

The greater of understanding we have of the fury of God's wrath towards sin, the greater value and appreciation we have for His mercy and salvation. As we read in Scripture about His holiness, righteousness, grace, and justification–let us not forget the great fires of hell that burn towards sin. Let us continually come before the Lord and kiss Him in our worship, knowing how great a salvation we have been given. We have left the kisses of betrayal behind and embrace the Son with great affection.

Day Eighteen

My Rights

I have been crucified with Christ; and it is no longer I who live, but Christ lives in me; and the life which I now live in the flesh I live by faith in the Son of God, who loved me and gave Himself up for me.
Galatians 2:20, NASB

Maybe you have heard this or even said something like this before. "I have rights." It interests me how bold and spoiled we can be as Christians. Remember, our *rights* are lost in Christ, as He gave Himself for us. In a society where everyone demands to be treated as equals; being treated as equals can only come when we see one another in the light of the cross. Remove the cross, and you remove the great leveler. Remove His blood, and you remove the fountain that washes prejudices away. Remove fellowship with the Holy Spirit, and you remove the one who unifies us into one chorus.

We have all sorts of demands. We demand and place expectations on others in the church, our pastors, the church service, church leadership. We want the best sounding worship. We want the most well-spoken pastor. We want money in our bank accounts. We want God to move in a way that is comfortable and not convicting. We want our order and not God's order. We don't want to be challenged to pursue God. We want to be the center of attention in our own way. We want control.

What filth we carry with us! What stench of pride arises from our hearts before a holy and pure God! And we are shocked that our churches and leaders are in such compromise. Let us remember that God sets the expectation. God has called us to holiness. God has sent His Spirit to remind us and convict us of all truth. God has called us to unity.

Here's a quote from Evangelist Steve Hill regarding the demands of God:

But what about God's demands? After all, He's the one who formed us in our mother's womb. He's the one who has given us life. God is the Master Potter and we are the earthen clay. He is the one we will give an account to. Therefore, it would be good to know what He demands of us. First of all, God demands a total allegiance to His person. That means He wants no other idols in your life. An idol is anything that takes the place of God in our lives. It can be sports, fame, or money. Jesus even spoke of loving God more than family. For many, that is a strong demand, but it must be obeyed. God also demands total allegiance to His cause. That means He expects you to spend your life speaking about His kingdom, not yours. He also demands total allegiance to holiness. "Without holiness," the Bible says, "no one will see the Lord" (Hebrews 12:14). It is not a suggestion that we be holy–it is a command. So next time demands are being made to God, make sure His demands are being met first.

Could it be that your demands of God are keeping you from experiencing His fullness? Today, your own assumptions and your own comfort could be hindering you from finding the best God has for you. Your demand that God move a certain way in your life, or a demand that God respect your own comfort and pride, could be blocking your breakthrough and leading you to a breakdown. Today is a great day to cease your striving over demands, and come humbly before God to receive all that He has for you!

Day Nineteen

Spiritual Intoxication

And do not be drunk with wine, in which is dissipation; but be filled with the Spirit
Ephesians 5:18, NKJV

Our society has become drunk on carnality. I'm not just speaking of alcohol but the entirety of carnal pleasures. Moderation is not even a consideration when it comes to the sin-saturated world in which we live.

When it comes to heavenly delights, there's no risk of overdoing it. You can delight yourself in God as much as you would like. We can never have too much of God. At no time does someone reach a place of having received all from the Lord there is to receive. At no time does the believer become so satisfied in God's boundless ocean of spiritual drink that he or she cannot take another indulgence.

Paul exhorts us to be filled, or "be being filled," in the Greek. This is a continual action. Drinking of the Lord's delights and goodness never cease. Solomon described this love of God as intoxicating.

Has the Lord's work had an inebriating effect on you? Drinking deeply of His joy will affect your happiness. Drinking deeply of His peace will affect your demeanor. Drinking deeply of His goodness will affect your attitude. Drinking deeply of His pleasures will affect what you find delight in.

Here's a glimpse from Sarah Edwards, wife of Jonathan Edwards, on drinking in the goodness of her Savior:

My safety and happiness and eternal enjoyment of God's immutable love seemed as durable and unchangeable as God Himself. Melted and overcome by the sweetness of this assurance, I fell into a great flow of tears and could not forbear weeping aloud. It appeared certain to me that God was my Father, and Christ my Lord and Savior, that He was mine and I His.

Under a delightful sense of the immediate presence and love of God, these words seemed to come over and over in my mind, 'My God, my all; my God, my all.' The presence of God was so near and so real that I seemed scarcely conscious of anything else. God the Father, and the Lord Jesus Christ, seemed as distinct persons, both manifesting their inconceivable loveliness and mildness and gentleness and their great and immutable love to me. I seemed to be taken under the care and charge of my God and Saviour, in an inexpressibly endearing manner; and Christ appeared to me as a mighty Saviour, under the character of the Lion of the tribe of Judah, taking my heart, with all its corruptions, under His care and putting it at His feet. In all things which concerned me I felt myself safe under the protection of the Father and the Saviour; who appeared with supreme kindness to keep a record of everything that I did, and of everything that was done to me, purely for my good.

Have another drink today of God's overwhelming pleasure. At His right hand are pleasures forevermore! (Psalm 16:11)

Day Twenty

Spiritual Songs

I will sing with the spirit, and I will also sing with the understanding.
1 Corinthians 14:15, NKJV

Throughout history, one of the characteristics of New Testament revival is songs of the Spirit. These are songs are spontaneous and unrehearsed. They are songs that erupt from a place of intimacy and worship. We have become a generation that is so programmed and performance driven that we often lack opportunity for spontaneous Spirit inspired songs. These are even more than semi-spontaneous phrases that are orchestrated ahead of time by the worship leader into a worship set list. It is actually quite silly how we attempt to even orchestrate how the Holy Spirit will move spontaneously.

The Azusa Street Revival was characterized by this spontaneous song of the Spirit. Here is how Frank Bartleman attempts to describe this song:

No one could understand this "gift of song" but those who had it. It was indeed a "new song" in the Spirit. When I first heard it in the meeting a great hunger entered my soul to receive it. I felt it would exactly express my pent-up feelings. I had not yet spoken in tongues. But the "new song" captured me. It was a gift from God of high order and appeared among us soon after the Azusa work began. No one had preached it. The Lord had sovereignly bestowed it, with the outpouring of the residue of oil, the latter rain baptism of the Spirit. It was exercised, as the Spirit moved the possessors, either in solo fashion, or by the company. It was sometimes without words, other times in tongues. The effect was wonderful on the people. It brought a heavenly atmosphere, as though the angels themselves were present and joining with us. And possible they were. It seemed to still criticism and opposition, and was hard for even wicked men to gainsay or ridicule.

We have experienced incredible songs of the Spirit in our ministry. It is tongues, English, and sounds of worship blended together in harmony. No person is leading this choir or taking credit for leading it, but certainly the Holy Spirit is inspiring the song. God seems to still us under His wings, and the gentle breeze of the Spirit brings forth this heavenly song of worship.

Singing in the Spirit requires nothing more than praying in the Spirit. It is a Spirit-inspired song. It is this wonderful language of intimacy set to a melody of inner worship and expressed in an outward way. Just as praying in tongues and in your natural language becomes a beautiful flow of fellowship and communion with God, spiritual songs become a worshipful flow of tongues and your natural language before the Lord.

Paul encourages us to sing out this "new song" to the Lord. Allow the same vocal chords that sing a written and understood song to sing out a spontaneous, heavenly song of worship. Soon you will find yourself lost in the glory of the one to whom you sing.

Day Twenty-One

No More Trash Talking

Death and life are in the power of the tongue
Proverbs 18:21, NKJV

Momma always said, "If you don't have anything nice to say, don't say anything at all." This might not be a quote from the Bible, but it's pretty powerful. One of the keys to maintaining an atmosphere of God's outpouring and revival is understanding the importance of the words we speak. Scripture is full of wisdom and revelation on the power of our words.

It seems as of late, social media and conversations are full of vile against the Church. And I hear it mostly from people who consider themselves a part of the Church. There are so many outside of the Body of Christ who would love to pick holes in the garments of the Church already. Why should we add to the nagging moth's work? Let's not destroy our own wedding garments! Imperfect as we all may be, we must contend for the Church and bless one another, not attack. We are to outdo one another in honor (Romans 12:10).

An element of this overflowing honor is to speak blessings, not curses. We must be people who speak the blessings of the Lord rather than the curses from our own flesh. Our natural response is to speak out of fear, rejection, hurt, insecurity, and other carnal motives. As believers, we are called higher — to speak blessings and life, not curses.

In Biblical history and in Jewish tradition, the power of speaking blessings is very powerful. Many Jewish families speak blessings over their children weekly. These blessings in Scripture oftentimes seem prophetic in nature, as we see their fulfillment looking back over time. But deeper than the prophetic nature, I believe it is the power of aligning our words with what God says about someone, not what our flesh sees about someone.

We see the power of blessing demonstrated as Jacob receives the blessing from Isaac rather than Esau. Esau wept and hated his brother when he discovered Isaac's blessing was bestowed on Jacob. Later in life Jacob blesses his own sons. You can find the account of Jacob's blessing of his sons in Genesis 49. The blessing bestowed on Joseph and his life are a great example of the almost prophetic nature of the blessing bestowed by Jacob.

Fast forward to the New Testament we are told to "bless those who curse you (Luke 6:28)." Paul writes in Romans to bless and not curse (Romans 12:14). In the Old Testament the blessing brought a sense of identity and purpose. In the New Testament, our identity and purpose are found in Christ. As we are found in Christ, we speak words of life, purpose, and identity. In John 12:49, Jesus says He speaks only what He hears from the Father.

What would happen if you spoke blessings and life, instead of speaking out of frustration, hurt, or anxiety? Recently in a prayer time with our worship team I began to bless them instead of just pray for them. As the spiritual leader of our spiritual house, I began to bless our team, and I watched them blossom like flowers. I watched as they opened up to receive the anointing I had just prayed that they would have.

In the course of ministry, I had a family that spoke negatively about me around their children. One day, one of the children faced a crisis, but the parents did not understand why the child was resistant to receiving from their pastor. Speaking curses had shut the family off from receiving the blessing from pastoral counsel. Repentance had to come before there could be breakthrough.

There's power in speaking blessings over your church, blessings over your pastors, blessings over your family, blessings over your children, blessings over your job! Be tuned in to what the Father is speaking, and say what He is saying. Speaking blessings will position you and others to walk in the fullness of God's plan and not lockdown the storehouses because of hurt, fear, and rejection. Instead of speaking out of fear and anxiety, ask the Lord what His Word says. Speak His Word instead of your own. Begin to speak blessings in faith, and the reward of faith will come!

Day Twenty-Two

From One Glory to the Next

But we all, with unveiled face, beholding as in a mirror the glory of the Lord, are being transformed into the same image from glory to glory, just as by the Spirit of the Lord.
2 Corinthians 3:18, NKJV

Revival is not a once-only occurrence, a set of good services, or a special event. To be revived and live in a place of awakening means to be continually stirred to the reality of heavenly things. Someone asked me recently about the outpouring in our church, "What's next?" Meaning– what's the agenda? How will this bring church growth? What's the formula? How does man get the glory?

I responded with, "This is it!" There is no next. God's glory is the objective. The presence of the Lord and His agenda is our agenda. I don't want anything else.

What God is doing is changing the hearts and lives of people. He's setting His church on fire for purity and power. He's snatching souls out of the pits of hell's eternal torment. There is no other agenda but to be changed from where we are now into who He wants us to be next.

God is constantly bringing us from one degree of glory to the next. As God is pouring out His Spirit, remember: There's always more. There's a new revelation of God's mercy for you. There's a new revelation of God's justice for you. There's a new revelation of God's love for you. There's a new revelation of God's goodness for you. There's a new revelation of God's provision for you. There's a new revelation of God's power for you. There's a new revelation of God's purity for you.

Should we lose our hunger for God and not foster our spiritual desires, Revivalist Charles Finney in *Experiencing Revival* gives us a glimpse of what might happen:

A revival will decline and cease unless Christians are frequently revived. By this I mean that Christians, in order to keep in the spirit of revival, need to be frequently convicted and humbled before God. The idea of a Christian being revived is something that many do not understand. But the fact is that, even during a revival, the Christian's heart is able to get crusted over and lose its exquisite desire for divine things. His anointing and prevalence in prayer abate, and he must be renewed again.

How do we maintain this precious gift that God has lavished upon us? We must live in a place of repentance and humility before the Lord, continually being transformed. We must allow the Holy Spirit to continually search our hearts and reveal the wickedness that keeps us from pressing in closer to the Lord. Let us never come to the place that says, "I've arrived." A taste of His glory leaves us wanting more, needing more, desperate for more. To drink of His glory stirs a longing to be transformed. To truly partake of His goodness leaves us wanting to be clean and spotless. To bask in His holiness brings an inward desire for this sanctifying presence to work deep in our own hearts — to be changed from our current status into the next.

What is the Lord transforming in you? Maybe He is releasing you from your past. The Lord might be breaking off the stubbornness and pride that lurks in the depths of your heart. He might be exposing hindrances to your fellowship with the Holy Spirit. He is creating His masterpiece within you that He might reveal this great glory through you.

I'm not satisfied with another service, another feeling, another great meeting. I must have Him! I must be changed to be like Him! What's next? To experience God in a greater degree that I might be like Him in a greater degree.

Day Twenty-Three

Can This Nation Live?

The hand of the Lord came upon me and brought me out in the Spirit of the Lord, and set me down in the midst of the valley; and it was full of bones. Then He caused me to pass by them all around, and behold, there were many in the open valley; and indeed they were very dry...Again He said to me, "Prophesy to these bones, and say to them, 'O dry bones, hear the word of the Lord!
Ezekiel 37:1-2, 4, NKJV

Many today are concerned with the state of our nation: politics, sin, war, nuclear threats, and so much more. Like Elijah, we must survey the reality of what lies in the valley. The stench of death fills the air. The bloodshed of innocence and purity has soaked the ground, and the only hope in sight is the awakening, reviving breath of God to blow again.

It is time for the church to rise and declare again the power of the Gospel. The Gospel is only good news if it can really transform. The Gospel is only powerful if the dead are raised to life. The fulfillment of Christ's death and resurrection means this Gospel is more than traditions of men—it is the power of God to salvation. It is the power of God over sickness and sin. It is the power of God to restore marriages and families. It is the power of God to change a nation—to change the world!

Here's a quote from Leonard Ravenhill from his book *Why Revival Tarries* concerning the valley Elijah saw:

Here was a curse – had he a cure? Here was death – could he bring life? This was no pretty declaration of doctrine. Dear believers, listen. The world is not waiting for a new definition of the Gospel, but for a new demonstration of the power of the Gospel. In these days of acute political helplessness, moral lawlessness, and spiritual helplessness, where are the men not of doctrine, but of faith? No faith is required to curse the darkness or give staggering statistical evidence that the dikes are down and a tidal wave of hellish impurity has submerged this generation. Doctrine? –we have enough and to spare, while a sick, sad, sin-sodden, sex-soaked world perishes with hunger. At this grim hour, the world sleeps in the darkness, and the Church sleeps in the light...

In this hour the Spirit of God is crying out, not for a great political leader or another great cause, He's crying out for truth and holiness in the Church. He's restoring the Church of Christ to purity and power. Jesus' anthem has not changed over the years:

But you shall receive power when the Holy Spirit has come upon you; and you shall be witnesses to Me in Jerusalem, and in all Judea and Samaria, and to the end of the earth.
Acts 1:8, NKJV

Step into your valley today with the boldness of the Spirit of God that came upon Elijah to prophesy over dead bones. Step into your valley today with the boldness of the Spirit of God that came upon David as he brought Goliath and the Philistines to their knees. The breath of the Spirit of God is blowing and awakening hearts today. The breath of the Spirit of God is blowing, making stones soar through the air and kill giants today.

Day Twenty-Four

Walking in Repentance and Revival

Repent therefore and be converted, that your sins may be blotted out, so that times of refreshing may come from the presence of the Lord
Acts 3:19, NKJV

During the Great Awakening, Pastor Jonathan Edwards was met with persecution and resistance concerning the divine happenings in the services. There were supernatural signs and wonders like spontaneous laughter and joy, people falling on the floor, shrieks and crying out, and the like. In an effort to bring Scriptural clarity, Edwards explained from 1 John 4:1, and other scriptures what God was doing. The sermon *The Distinguishing Marks of a Work of the Spirit of God* is a great message and worth reading today.

Let me highlight some of Edwards's excerpts from the applications of this message:

1. The recent extraordinary influence is from the Spirit of God.
The Spirit who is at work takes people's minds off vanities of the world. He engages them in a deep concern about eternal happiness. He puts their thoughts on earnestly seeking their salvation. He convinces them of the dreadfulness of sin, their own guile, and miserable natural state.

2. We should do our utmost to promote it.
We should not oppose or do anything in the least to clog or hinder the work. On the contrary, we should do our utmost to promote it. Now Christ is come down from heaven in a remarkable and wonderful work of His Spirit. It is proper for all His professed disciples to acknowledge Him and give Him honor.

3. Friends of this work must give diligent heed to themselves.
Let me earnestly exhort such to give diligent heed to themselves. Avoid all errors and misconduct. Avoid whatever may darken and obscure the work. Give no occasion to those who stand ready to reproach it...Humility, self-denial, and an entire dependence on our Lord Jesus Christ will be our best defense. Let us therefore maintain the strictest watch against spiritual pride. Let us avoid being lifted up with extraordinary experiences and comforts. Let us not take pride in the high favors of heaven that any of us may have received. We need these favors in a special manner in order to keep a strict and jealous eye upon our

own hearts. Pride is the worst viper in the heart. It is the first sin that ever entered into the universe. It lies lowest of all in the foundation of the whole building of sin. Of all lusts, it is the most secret, deceitful, and unsearchable in its ways of working. It is ready to mix with everything. Nothing is so hateful to God, contrary to the spirit of the Gospel, or of so dangerous consequence. There is no one sin that does so much to let the devil into the hearts of the saints and expose them to his delusions. Now is the time for another Awakening that will transform our country and the world. The rains of revival and renewal are falling. Embrace what the Lord is doing and be changed by Him! Allow your devotion to deepen and your pride to be purged. Shout from the rooftops the work of the Lord!

Day Twenty-Five

Immersed into God

As for me, I baptize you with water for repentance, but He who is coming after me is mightier than I, and I am not fit to remove His sandals; He will baptize you with the Holy Spirit and fire.
Matthew 3:11, NASB

The continual crowds had gathered outside of the city to hear John the Baptist preach his message of repentance, and they were baptized by him. Even the religious vipers had gathered to hear this message with unrepentant hearts. This was new. It was a similar yet different message. It was a sermon preached in a different location. Instead of finely dressed religious leaders pontificating, a man dressed in camel's hair clothes was declaring the message of the Kingdom. It was a similar but very different season. Something was happening, and those who were spiritually aware received!

John was baptizing to repentance, but there was one coming who would immerse people into the very presence of God. This baptism of repentance was followed by a baptism of His presence, His power, and His purity.

John 14:16
I will ask the Father, and He will give you another Helper, that He may be with you forever

Acts 1:8
but you will receive power when the Holy Spirit has come upon you; and you shall be My witnesses both in Jerusalem, and in all Judea and Samaria, and even to the remotest part of the earth.

John 14:26
But the Helper, the Holy Spirit, whom the Father will send in My name, He will teach you all things, and bring to your remembrance all that I said to you.

This baptism of fire that John spoke of was cleansing, fortifying, and intensifying. It would bring to the surface the impurities that lay within the repentant heart. It would melt away the hardness of spiritual apathy. The fire of God would set ablaze the altar of one's life to burn for Christ. This Holy Spirit fire would set the mouth of its recipient on fire with worship, prayer, and the bold message of the Word.

53

We are to be continually immersed into God and His cleansing fire. At no time do we find ourselves fully purged, and at no time is the flame of our passion as great as God's passion for His own glory. We continually lack with regards to Christ, and thus we must be continually filled. Continually, we must be immersed for cleansing. Continually, we must be immersed for passion. Continually, we must be immersed for power. Continually, we must be immersed for righteousness. Continually, we must be immersed for peace. Continually, we must be immersed for joy. This is what Paul declared in Ephesians 5:18. We must be continually filled!

Today is a great day to be immersed into God. Be baptized into His Spirit. Drink deeply of His love. Just as John the Baptist laid his hands on them and placed them under the water of the Jordan, let Christ place His hands upon you and place you under the flow of His Spirit.

Day Twenty-Six

How to Receive Correction

So Moses' father-in-law said to him, "The thing that you do is not good. Both you and these people who are with you will surely wear yourselves out. For this thing is too much for you; you are not able to perform it by yourself. Listen now to my voice; I will give you counsel, and God will be with you: Stand before God for the people, so that you may bring the difficulties to God. And you shall teach them the statutes and the laws, and show them the way in which they must walk and the work they must do. Moreover, you shall select from all the people able men, such as fear God, men of truth, hating covetousness; and place such over them to be rulers of thousands, rulers of hundreds, rulers of fifties, and rulers of tens. And let them judge the people at all times. Then it will be that every great matter they shall bring to you, but every small matter they themselves shall judge. So it will be easier for you, for they will bear the burden with you. If you do this thing, and God so commands you, then you will be able to endure, and all this people will also go to their place in peace." So Moses heeded the voice of his father-in-law and did all that he had said.
Exodus 18:17-24, NKJV

1. Humble yourself and avoid the prideful responses.
Moses was "called" of God to lead the Israelites; "surely he knew best how to shepherd them" (sarcasm added). Many times, our pride will lead us quickly down a path of destruction (Prov 16:18) that in actuality we really do not want to journey down. It is amazing how quickly we can allow ourselves to be caught in the cycle of justification, deflection, excuses, lying, and simply, pure conflict due to our pride.

Moses listened and responded graciously. "So Moses heeded the voice of his father-in-law and did all that he had said." Moses did not try to "save face" or cover up the reality; he simply humbled himself to receive wisdom. The wisdom he received bore witness with him and the leading of God in his life, and the process of implementation began.

Protection comes from submission to the appropriate, God-appointed leadership in your life. Even if you "feel" absolutely correct in your own judgment, God may have something else for you to learn and grow into. Moses would not continue in leadership successfully had he not learned this valuable lesson from a timely rebuke.

2. Follow the Lord's direction.
Moses truly had a calling from God to lead the Israelites. Moses met with

God face to face. God could have revealed this great leadership truth in their alone time together; however, God chose to use Moses' father-in-law to speak truth in a timely manner. God given correction will reflect to you the purposes of God's calling and refine you for continued fulfillment of this calling. Moses recognized he was running thin on energy and carrying an emotional and spiritual load he was not intended to carry; he simply needed godly wisdom and direction from a third party. Imagine Moses's new-found effectiveness after implementing his father-in-law's advice.

3. Obedience to correction is a gift to others.
As a result of Moses submitting to and honoring God by honoring his father-in-law, the Israelites were blessed: New leaders were born, the people learned to self-govern, Moses was refreshed, and the new leaders grew in maturity and discernment. Such are the results of the blessing of correction. Often times we can also learn from other's corrections and mistakes. When walking in humility, we learn to extend grace to others from the same grace of which we have received.

4. Honor those with a different vantage point.
Correction can be difficult to receive. Our pride and ambition can get the best of us. We have to place it in check, and let humility begin to lead us. Then, we must honor those who come with correction. Moses did not leave the meeting with his father-in-law and begin to share personal frustrations and "family only" drama. He honored his father-in-law by heeding his advice and utilizing his wisdom for implementation. Exodus 18:27, states that, "Moses let his father-in-law depart" after implementation. In other words, Moses honored the correction and followed through by seeking his father-in-law's continued assistance until the corrective action was carried out.

This place of humility and honor brings the Lord's blessing and peace to everyone involved. Long-term relationships can be continued from a place of honor. Neglect of this honor can cause unnecessary tension and future faction.

Day Twenty-Seven

Don't Eat Your Seed

Now may He who supplies seed to the sower, and bread for food, supply and multiply the seed you have sown and increase the fruits of your righteousness, while you are enriched in everything for all liberality, which causes thanksgiving through us to God.
2 Corinthians 9:10-11, NKJV

All finances and resources God places into our hands contain seed for sowing and bread for eating. Be careful not to eat your seed, or there will be no future harvest. With every blessing, the Lord provides for our needs, and He gives us additional blessing to give away. Before you can receive what is in God's hand, you must first "sow" what is in your hand.

In the preceding verse (v. 8), Paul writes, *And God is able to make all grace abound toward you, that you, always having all sufficiency in all things, may have an abundance for every good work.* He is connecting seed for sowing and bread for eating to our liberality in giving.

In the Greek, "all sufficiency," means "everything needed to sustain your life." God is able to provide all we need to sustain life. Remember, Jesus taught us not to worry about what we would wear or how we would maintain our life. As believers, we are now heavenly citizens with a God who cares and supplies.

Beyond meeting our needs, Paul says that God will also give us *an abundance for every good work.* In other words, God is able to take care of our needs but also give us lavish overflow to support the work of God.

Scripture clearly teaches us, and it is again stated here, that God releases finances into the hands of His people to steward the work of the Kingdom in the earth. When we walk in the principles God has placed before us, we walk in blessing in our personal lives and have overflow for the work of God. No longer do we operate under the curse of the law, squandering our resources on unrighteous living, but we have been given the ability to get wealth to be generous.

Farmers do not eat their seed. They work to maintain the soil that produces healthy and abundant crops. They are looking for opportunity to sow seed in order that they may have additional seeds and additional crops. For the believer, giving should not be a struggle but an easy overflow of the work of God in us. We should be looking for opportunities to support the work of God in this life, which makes eternal investments in the next.

Have you experience a lack of increase in your life? Do you feel like every time you get ahead something else is eating your resources? Have you considered the seed your sowing? Are you misappropriating resources that should be designated as seed into God's soil? Every seed contains a miracle, but the seed has to go into the soil for the miracle to manifest.

To simply assume the resources God has given are only for enjoyment in this life is misdirected worship. We are now worshiping this life and resources, versus the giver and His eternal purposes. If we steward our resources better, consider how much farther and quicker the Gospel could go into the deepest corners of the earth. The harvest field is ripe with souls. The harvest workers are called and ready to labor. Sowing your seed in the Kingdom enables the Gospel workers to go forth and brings blessing into your life.

Day Twenty-Eight

Giant or Grasshopper

There we saw the giants; and we were like grasshoppers in our own sight, and so we were in their sight.
Numbers 13:33, NKJV

Have you ever faced a seemingly insurmountable task or opposition? I'm sure we all have faced circumstances that seem impossible in the natural. In this Scripture, Moses sent out spies into the Promised Land. We know that ten of the twelve spies came back with a negative report, but Joshua and Caleb were ready to conquer every giant and take possession of their promises. Here are a couple thoughts as you encounter the giants of life. Remember, our God is not a grasshopper; He is bigger than every giant you could face!

1. The same God that gives you access and favor behind the enemy lines will give you the victory over your circumstance.
The spies, obviously shorter in stature than the current occupants, were able to move freely behind enemy lines and spy out the land. This presents an obvious issue. The Israelite spies are clearly outsiders and yet are able to determine the inhabitability of the land and the military strength of their enemy.

2. We do not shrink back in fear, but we advance to conquer.
Hebrews 10:29 says that we are not of those who turn away or shrink back but of those who have faith and advance. The spies with the bad report reverted back to their old life of slavery and torture. They forgot the possibilities and were trapped by fear. Fear will always keep you in the land of what was and out of what can be.

3. God is a Promise Keeper not a Manipulator
God did not bring the Israelites this far on their journey to the Promised Land to leave them stranded. God does not manipulate us out of fear and guilt, He brings us out to bring us in. God always exchanges our worst for His best; our sin for His righteousness; our insignificance for His identity. Consider even our tithe: God receives ten percent and exchanges it for bountiful blessing.

4. As a Man Thinks, so is He
The spies reported of their small stature: We were like grasshoppers. Your life, in view of the great possibilities ahead, may cause your

insecurities to arise and your stature in Christ to diminish. Maybe God has called you to step out of something old to enter into something new, and the possibility is overwhelming. The spies said we were like grasshoppers *in our own sight*. How the spies saw themselves became the report they shared with others. How do you identify yourself? Are you trusting in a God that is able to kill the giants, or do you view Him as a grasshopper? Begin to magnify God today in worship, and see Him as bigger than any circumstance you face. It's time to see through eyes of faith and not fear.

Day Twenty-Nine

Seedtime & Harvest

Then Isaac sowed in that land [in the time of famine], and reaped in the same year a hundredfold; and the Lord blessed him. The man began to prosper, and continued prospering until he became very prosperous
Genesis 26:12-13, NKJV

Throughout life and Christianity, we see the relentless principle of sowing and reaping. There are many scriptures that reference the power of seedtime and harvest. Here are two:

Do not be deceived, God is not mocked; for whatever a man sows, that he will also reap. (Galatians 6:7, NKJV)

Now may He who supplies seed to the sower, and bread for food, supply and multiply the seed you have sown and increase the fruits of your righteousness (2 Corinthians 9:10, NKJV)

Isaac found himself living in a time of famine. Famine describes a season of lack, pestilence, illness, starvation, dehydration, economic downfall, and financial hardship-- among other things. Famine is not a term we like to hear, and we certainly do not want to experience it. In Genesis, Isaac demonstrates for us the two separate economic systems the believer experiences:

1.) The world's system which is under the curse of the law (that we have been redeemed from) and 2.) God's system that is heavenly in origin.

Isaac chose to live according to God's system of economics in the time of lack. Faith sows seed when, in the natural, you want to stockpile. God's economy has never operated on the stockpile method but has always operated in generosity.

The generous soul will be made rich, and he who waters will also be watered himself. (Proverbs 11:25, NKJV)

Because Isaac trusted the Lord, he became very prosperous. He was so prosperous that the Philistines envied him. Is it possible that God desires to prosper your life in such a way that the unbelieving see the goodness of God overflowing in your life? Is your time of lack keeping you from sowing seed generously? Our God is not a stingy God, and He desires to abundantly bless His children.

We know that unfaithfulness in our tithe invites a curse on our finances. We understand that unless the seed is sown, no harvest can be produced. However, many times out of fear, forgetfulness, or pride we do not sow and miss out on the harvest that follows. Many people want the blessing of the Lord on their finances and yet do not sow their seed.

Here are some thoughts regarding your financial seeds and God's promised harvest:

1. All finances God places into your hands contain SEED for sowing and BREAD for eating. Be careful not to eat your seed, or there will be no future harvest. (2 Corinthians 9:10)
2. Every seed contains a miracle, but the miracle only happens when the seed is sown. (Proverbs 3:9-10)
3. Only God can produce the harvest. We are responsible for sowing and receiving. (1 Corinthians 3:6)
4. The righteous live under the blessing of God, and have been redeemed from the curse of law. Righteous living brings the blessing. (Galatians 3:13; Deuteronomy 28:1-14)
5. Your source of income is about more than putting food on the table. It is an opportunity for the Kingdom to advance in the earth. "I make a living to be a giver." Every seed sown into God's Kingdom affects someone's life. (Philippians 1:1-8)
6. Financial deposits are credited to your heavenly account as you sow your seed. God takes notice of every seed sown, and His accounting is perfect. (Philippians 4:17; Luke 21:1-4)
7. Know the difference between seed and need. If He's not meeting a need, there must be seed. (Matthew 6:31-33)
8. Your harvest is in proportion to the seed sown. (2 Corinthians 9:6)
9. Be willing to give away what is of temporary value to gain something of eternal value. (Matthew 6:19-21)
10. Faith in God to protect, provide, and preserve you releases you from fear of lack and the control of poverty. (Philippians 4:19; Psalm 122:7)

Day Thirty

The Way Maker

I will go before you and make the crooked places straight; I will break in pieces the gates of bronze and cut the bars of iron. I will give you the treasures of darkness and hidden riches of secret places, that you may know that I, the Lord, who call you by your name, am the God of Israel.
Isaiah 45:2-3, NKJV

Growing up I would go with my grandparents to visit my great grandparents in the backwoods of Missouri. To this day, I can remember the up and down hilly roads that were winding and twisting through the seemingly endless forest of trees. One wrong move and the car could be off the side of the road and down the embankment. As a child, I had so much fun going on those winding and hilly roads because I would get the roller coaster feeling in the bottom of my stomach. Somehow, I don't think my grandparents got as much enjoyment from the ride.

Life can be as full of winding, twisting, ups and downs and those roads of uncertainty. Maybe you have felt the nearness of the danger that lurks around the next corner of life. Maybe you have experienced confusion and uncertainty along the journey.

Isaiah prophesies here about the majestic character and ability of our God not only to handle, but to overcome any obstacle we face. He truly is the Way Maker in our lives. Blessed is the man or woman whom God goes before. He promises not only to handle the crooked places, but He promises to go before us and guide us through whatever life may bring along our journey. As we face those uncertain times, He makes confusion cease to clarity. He makes turmoil cease to peace. He make obstacles break forth into opportunities.

Through every circumstance, we can have childlike faith, trusting that not only God is at the wheel of our lives, but He is the author and the finisher of our lives. Not only has God gone before us, but He directs every circumstance we face. Crooked places and obstacles are assured but so is the sovereign hand of God's providence through them all.

Behind every crooked place and every obstacle are secret riches. The riches of which God speaks may include blessings in this life, but greater than these are the riches of knowing the Lord who is calling your name. In the darkness and uncertainty, His voice brings clarity and peace. His voice stills the troubled waters. His voice instructs in the way that we should go. His voice speaks life and light to the darkness. Jesus said that His sheep know His voice. How blessed we are to know Him more intimately during the uncertainties of life.

Consider the sifting that Peter would face at Christ's death. Jesus spoke to Peter that He would endure the trial and on the other side would encourage others in Christ. Even knowing the hardships Peter would go through, knowing the betrayal that would come — Christ was confident in His prayer to the Father to sustain Peter through it all. Jesus is interceding for you today. As one with the Father, He is confident in His prayer that our lives will be preserved through whatever we face. We haven't earned this consideration or deserve His preservation. It is simply because of the Father's great love!

Next time you are facing twisting, winding, hilly roads of confusion and uncertainty, or obstacles seem to be blocking your progress, have assurance. Your God, who has gone before you, is revealing Himself mighty and strong on your behalf. He is the Way Maker for you!

Day Thirty-One

It's Time to Dream

When the Lord brought back the captive ones of Zion, we were like those who dream. Then our mouth was filled with laughter and our tongue with joyful shouting
Psalm 126:1-2a, NASB

Do you ever feel like you have lost your ability to dream? Maybe you no longer have God's direction and purpose for your life? I often think of Joseph who had a God-given purpose and direction. He continued to dream despite the jealousy and taunting of his brothers. Sometimes our God-given dreams bring us to places where we find ourselves, like Joseph, in the pit of despair, in bondage as a slave, and sorting through slanderous accusations. Sometimes we wonder if we, like Ebenezer Scrooge, had some bad cheese when we "thought" we heard from God. Have you been there? Maybe you are in a place like this today. The direction you thought your life was going seemingly took a wrong turn.

What do captivity, wilderness journeys, accusations, and trials all have in common with God-dreams? According to James, various kinds of trials and afflictions are headed your way when you begin to yield to God's direction for your life. Rather than become discouraged and weary, we have an opportunity to rejoice and know that the same God who called us to the journey will lead us through.

The greatest place of joy, I believe, is walking through the storms with Christ. We can no longer rely on our own strength, and so the joy of the Lord must become our strength. Through the trial, we understand our inability to change our circumstance, and our only resolve is to be joyful in the Lord.

Determine you will not stop dreaming no matter the circumstance. Like John in Revelation, get caught up in the Spirit and overflow with the joyful revelation of Christ. John was boiled in oil and exiled on an island. Circumstances like that can certainly prevent us from dreaming, but they can also be the catalyst for things never seen or experienced before.

I love what Charles Spurgeon writes about this Psalm:

So full were they of joy that they could not contain themselves. They must express their joy and yet they could not find expression for it. Irrepressible mirth could do no other than laugh, for speech was far too dull a thing for it. The mercy was so unexpected, so amazing, so singular that they could not do less than laugh; and they laughed much, so that their mouths were full of it, and that because their hearts were full too. When at last the tongue could move articulately, it could not be content simply to talk, but it must needs sing; and sing heartily too, for it was full of singing. Doubtless the former pain added to the zest of the pleasure; the captivity threw a brighter color into the emancipation. The people remembered this joy flood for years after, and here is the record of it turned into a song. Note the when and the then. God's when is our then. At the moment when he turns our captivity, the heart turns from its sorrow; when he fills us with grace we are filled with gratitude. We were made to be as them that dream, but we both laughed and sang in our sleep.

Day Thirty-Two

A New Chapter

The Lord's loving kindnesses indeed never cease, for His compassions never fail.
They are new every morning; Great is Your faithfulness.
Lamentations 3:23, NASB

Great is the Lord's faithfulness. It is because of His compassions we are
not consumed. It is because of His great mercies we can have wonderful
new life daily. Every morning you can wake up and breathe the air of
His faithful compassion.

It's time to enjoy a new chapter. Determine today that you will yield to
God, and as you do, cooperate with Him as He unfolds the story of your
life. You do not have to continue in the chapters of yesterday's news, but
allow Him in His great compassion and mercies to bring something fresh
to the storybook pages.

Lamentations 3:24 says: *The Lord is my portion*. As we taste of the
goodness of God, He truly is all we need. His compassions sustain us,
provide for us, and protect us. When looking at the hungry multitudes,
Jesus was moved with compassion, not because they were hungry, but
because they were like sheep without a shepherd. Today, His
compassion is shepherding you and guiding you to still waters that can
restore your soul.

Here is what Matthew Henry has said concerning this compassion of
God:

Bad as things are, it is owing to the mercy of God that they are not worse. We
should observe what makes for us, as well as what is against us. God's
compassions fail not; of this we have fresh instances every morning. Portions on
earth are perishing things, but God is a portion forever. It is our duty, and will
be our comfort and satisfaction, to hope and quietly to wait for the salvation of
the Lord. If we cannot say with unwavering voice, "The Lord is my portion";
may we not say, "I desire to have Him for my portion and salvation, and in his
word do I hope?" Happy shall we be, if we learn to receive affliction as laid upon
us by the hand of God.

Oh, how bountiful and happy are the compassions of the Lord! What
compassion He has throughout the ages that we might discover His
riches. It requires no compassion to prevent hardship. But great is the

compassion of God that allows His children to be brought to hardship, sustained through it, and brought out as refined gold. Great are His compassions that allow the testing and proving of our faith that we might be lacking in no good thing. Great are His compassions that restrain His sovereign hand from ceasing the turbulence in order that we might see Him walking on the water in the midst of the storm!

Allow the Compassionate King to begin something new in you today. Whether through the storm, in the valley below, or on the mountaintop above; let us sing of His wonderful mercy. After all, it is a new day, and His mercies are new every morning!

Day Thirty-Three

Created for Communion

He who did not spare His own Son, but delivered Him up for us all, how shall He not with Him also freely give us all things?
Romans 8:32, NKJV

Leonard Ravenhill once shared a conversation he had with A.W. Tozer:

I think again of a statement A.W. Tozer made to me once. He said, "Len, you know, we'll hardly get our feet out of time into eternity that we'll bow our heads in shame and humiliation. We'll gaze on eternity and say, 'Look at all the riches there were in Jesus Christ, and I've come to the Judgment Seat almost a pauper.'" For God had not only given us Jesus Christ – He has with Him freely given us all things.

We were born for divine fellowship. We were intentionally designed spirit, soul, and body to have communion with God as humans. After all, Christ came to restore us back to God, and now divine communication should be a part of our daily life. How do you start your day? I'm not talking about how much time you spend reading the Word or how many chapters of the Bible you read. Before your feet hit the ground, are you aware of God in your life? Do you greet Him in the morning? Do you think about Him before you go to sleep? Most of us never give much thought to divine communion except for Sundays, and if we do, it's out of need. I wonder what would happen if someone you cared about deeply only spoke to you when they needed something.

We were made for continual communication with the Creator of all things. As believers we rejoice that we are born again. We thank God for Jesus who became our sacrifice and took the punishment of our sin. However, Christianity does not end there. That's where it begins. The New Testament writers describe this continual communication and life with God.

Consider what Paul says in 1 Thessalonians 5:23: *May your whole spirit, soul and body be preserved blameless...* We are intricately designed as a tripartite creation. Consider the tabernacle of the Old Testament and how it was comprised likewise: outer court, inner court, and holy of holies. The outer court is our bodies which contain our senses. The inner court is our soul which contains our mind, will, and emotions; and the holy of holies is our spirit person. We are spirits who have souls and live in bodies. God dwells in the spirit, the "self" dwells in the soul, and the senses dwell in the body.

In the world in which we live, we spend more time and energy on our natural man—the soul and body. Often, we do not nurture and develop our spirit man. Our spirit man is where communion with God begins. This is not to say we are to ignore our soul and body. Paul says that all three should be preserved blameless. This is why we need the fullness of the Spirit in all areas of our lives.

Our body must be disciplined, and our soul must be sanctified. Our body is offered as a sacrifice of worship, and our soul must be transformed from glory to glory. Our spirit man must continually be nourished by feasting on God and drinking of the waters of life (Ephesians 5:18). This journey of discipleship, sanctification, drinking, and feasting are living a life in communion with God.

Day Thirty-Four

Katalambano

May be able to comprehend with all the saints what is the width and length and depth and height – to know the love of Christ which passes knowledge; that you may be filled with all the fullness of God.
Ephesians 3:18-19, NKJV

In Ephesians 3:18, Paul uses this Greek word, which is interpreted in the NKJV as "comprehend." Oftentimes, we lose a lot in translation from Hebrew and Greek to English. This is one of those words that loses its gusto in translation. The definition of *Katalambano* is "to lay hold of so as to make one's own; to take possession of; apprehend."

Paul is praying that you and I would be able to lay hold of the vastness of God's love. He goes on to say that this love is so vast, you cannot understand it in the natural; the greatness of God's love is only understood with spiritual understanding. Have you ever thought about the expanse of the heavens? The heavens cannot even begin to contain God, and so, the vastness of God's love supersedes anything we even attempt to comprehend. As believers, no matter how much of the love of God we have experienced, there are still vast oceans of rich love divine. Launch out!

One of my other favorite Bible words is used in the same text: "Ginosko." Paul tells us we need to apprehend this great love and make it our own, and then, we are to "know it by experience." It is possible to have knowledge that something is true, but it is quite different to experience that truth. For example, Jonathan Edwards often used the analogy of knowing that honey is sweet, but when you taste and see, there is a new depth to the sweetness of honey. We can know the Lord is sweet, but when you taste the sweetness for yourself, there is new depth to your understanding.

God has a reservoir of love that "passes knowledge." It exceeds and excels beyond anything we can begin to think or imagine. Today, He calls us to make every effort to passionately pursue and enjoy this eternal supply of love. Discovering your pleasures in the oceans of His love will satisfy you more fully than any earthly treasure and yet will leave you longing for more of Him.

It has been said and sung, but how true these words are:

Could we with ink the ocean fill, and were the skies of parchment made; were every stalk on earth a quill, and every man a scribe by trade; to write the love of God above, would drain the ocean dry; nor could the scroll contain the whole, though stretched from sky to sky. The love of God, how rich and pure! How measureless and strong. It shall forevermore endure the saints and angel's song.

It is time to launch out into the depths of His love. Let nothing hinder or hold you back on the shore of comfort and complacency. It is in the ocean's depths that you behold the wonders of God. Determine that you will apprehend and take possession of this one thing—God's love. Make it your life's aim and your single passion to know the depths of His amazing love.

Day Thirty-Five

Heavenly Capital

"Moreover, when you fast, do not be like the hypocrites, with a sad countenance. For they disfigure their faces that they may appear to men to be fasting. Assuredly, I say to you, they have their reward. But you, when you fast, anoint your head and wash your face, so that you do not appear to men to be fasting, but to your Father who is in the secret place; and your Father who sees in secret will reward you openly. "Do not lay up for yourselves treasures on earth, where moth and rust destroy and where thieves break in and steal; but lay up for yourselves treasures in heaven, where neither moth nor rust destroys and where thieves do not break in and steal. For where your treasure is, there your heart will be also.
Matthew 6:16-21, NKJV

In this passage of Scripture, Jesus is relating the power of prayer and fasting to our heavenly treasures. Many times, we use Matthew 6:19-21 as an instruction for offerings, which is valuable; however, Jesus connects prayer and our heavenly investment. In *Why Revival Tarries*, Ravenhill says, "Prayer is to the believer what capital is to the businessman."

Capital in this sense is wealth or property that is used or invested to produce more wealth. Capital is also the money with which a business is started. Our prayer life is one of the investments we make into our heavenly bank account, and the return on our investment is souls. We sow intercession and reap changed lives.

Jude 1:23 says we ought to snatch men's souls from the fire. In our prayer time, we are affected by the Holy Spirit to intercede on behalf of the lost, we receive supernatural compassion for the lost, and we receive urgency for the hour.

Having a consistent prayer life is less about presenting your checklist of "needs and wants" before God, but rather depositing a heavenly investment for eternal rewards. The more you pray, the more you deposit. The more you pray, the more the Holy Spirit imparts compassion and urgency for the lost. The more you pray, the more you begin to participate in a life of evangelism. The more you pray, the more return in souls saved you will see. Who are you praying for today? How can you spend more time in passionate prayer for the lost?

Revelation describes the bowls storing up the saint's intercession. Think about the power of your prayers in this context. As you pray, these intercessions ascend to the heavens as incense before God, and they are filling your bowl of prayer. The answers to these prayers are sent with the fire off God's altar. Is your intercession bowl tipping over with the weighty prayers of God's desires and passions, or is there barely enough prayers to need a bowl at all?

He sends His fire as we pray. The fire from the altar of God comes in direct proportion to the prayers that are filling the bowl of our intercession. James tells us that it is the prayers of the righteous that make God's power available (James 5:16). Much like connecting a light into a power outlet, we must be connected to God's power through prayer. It is there, in prayer, that the fire falls.

Day Thirty-Six

Plenteous Power

Confess your trespasses to one another, and pray for one another, that you may be healed. The effective, fervent prayer of a righteous man avails much.
James 5:16, NKJV

James 5:16 in The Amplified Bible says: *The earnest (heartfelt, continued) prayer of a righteous man makes tremendous power available [dynamic in its working].*

The Greek paints a very clear picture of the tremendous power made available to us when we pray. Using the Greek, here is a word picture I use to describe this power: *A passionately engaged petition before God becomes like an electrical wire for power to flow through to a shining light: making abundant, overflowing, and plenteous power available.*

The Gospel is the power of God that brings salvation (Romans 1:16). Jesus' death and resurrection makes this power accessible to us. Your prayer life is the wire which God's power can flow through into your life and out of your life. The Holy Spirit is the person who makes this power effective in our lives. Your life is like the light bulb; the effectiveness of your light bulb is directly related to the amount of time you spend in prayer—and not just the amount, but the quality of that time.

James includes in his writing, "the heartfelt, earnest, passionately engaged" prayer is tremendously effective. What is the "blood pressure" of your prayer life? Is the output and gauge of your prayer life at a place to sustain vibrant Christianity?

It is God's intention that believers are overflowing with supernatural power. As you connect to this power today through prayer, allow His power to flow vibrantly into and through your life.

And when God sends us on His great embassy, He pledges Himself to enable us to carry it out successfully. This promise of power just means all we need for efficiency. It is sufficiency for efficiency, all personal qualifications, providential workings and divine enablings that we have a right to expect for the successful accomplishment of the work that is given us to do. (A.B. Simpson)

Set before believers is the greatest purpose anyone can ever be given: The redemption of mankind. For such a great labor, there is great power made available. God has not sent us without experience, without resource, without understanding, or without power. To the degree one is willing to commit to this great purpose, there is an even greater supply from God. Knowing Christ and the power of His resurrection will overflow in making His resurrection and His power known to others. The discovery of this power and the use of the overflow of God's power in ministry to others is a result of time in prayer and fellowship with Him.

Day Thirty-Seven

A Divine & Supernatural Light

Arise, shine; For your light has come! And the glory of the Lord is risen upon you. For behold, the darkness shall cover the earth, and deep darkness the people; But the Lord will arise over you, and His glory will be seen upon you. The Gentiles shall come to your light, and kings to the brightness of your rising.
Isaiah 60:1-3, NKJV

In this passage of Scripture, we find this radiant, supernatural light — the divine glory of God — radiating over and from His people. In the midst of a dark and wayward society, the importance of God's supernatural light is all the more paramount. As the darkness of this world grows even darker, the glory of the Lord within His church is growing brighter and more vibrant.

When we face days of despair around us, let us not grow weary in well doing (Galatians 6:9), for the harvest of the ages is assured and is nearer than we can begin to anticipate. Those who have lost their way, those who are in bondage to darkness, and those who have been lost will be drawn to this radiant light of the glory of God.

Hebrews tells us that Christ is the radiance of the Father (Hebrews 1:3). In Christ, we see this perfect glory made manifest. Jesus said that the Holy Spirit would glorify Him and make known to us the Father (John 16:14). How does God's glory increase in our lives? By yielding to this wonderful person, the Holy Spirit. As we learn to walk in the Spirit, we will not fulfill the deeds of darkness, rather we will radiate the glory of God (Galatians 5:16). Ask God today to help you radiate the glory of God through the power of the Holy Spirit.

This light gives a view of those things that are immensely the most exquisitely beautiful, and capable of delighting the eye of understanding. This spiritual light is the dawning of the light of glory in the heart. There is nothing so powerful as this to support persons in affliction, and to give the mind peace and brightness, in this stormy and dark world. (Jonathan Edwards)

The rousing up and reviving of believers is not a small matter; it concerns the glory of God. If the lamps do not shine, it does not speak well for the oil, nor of the care of the keeper. And if the children of God do not testify for Him, it does not speak well for their High Priest in heaven, nor for the Holy Spirit within them. (Andrew Bonar)

As a believer, you are a child of the Light and distinctly different. You have been brought out of darkness, filled with oil, and set on fire to burn as a beacon in the darkness. Light is fully in contrast with darkness. We have been sent to shine, not to be flickering and dim. Lights in the midst of darkness are opposite of the current culture. Lights in the midst of darkness are challenging and convicting to that darkness. Lights in the midst of darkness are not taking on the nature of darkness in order to reach the darkness. Lights in the midst of darkness are different and are meant to be so. You are meant to stand out, look different, live different, and challenge the status quo. You are not the average person filled with darkness. You are alive and filled with light to shine in the midst of despair. Let your light shine before others today that they might see Christ!

Day Thirty-Eight

The Tabernacle of David

"On that day I will raise up the tabernacle of David, which has fallen down, and repair its damages; I will raise up its ruins, and rebuild it as in the days of old; That they may possess the remnant of Edom, and all the Gentiles who are called by My name," Says the LORD who does this thing. "Behold, the days are coming," says the LORD, "When the plowman shall overtake the reaper, and the treader of grapes him who sows seed; The mountains shall drip with sweet wine, and all the hills shall flow with it.
Amos 9:11-13, NKJV

We are living in an urgent hour. The time of Christ's return is upon us and there are souls hanging in the balance of eternity. As Jonathan Edwards has said, "the bow of God's wrath is bent and the arrow made ready on the string, and justice bends the arrow of your heart and strains the bow." In these days, God is restoring the tabernacle of His Glory — a dwelling place in the hearts and lives of any who will yield their lives to Him.

David's tabernacle, referenced in Amos 9, was a place of perpetual worship. It was a place where the presence of God was known to dwell and where lives were transformed. David's tabernacle did not contain the splendor and riches of Solomon's temple. No, it was a tattered tent. But greater than the glory of its furnishings, was the Ark of the Covenant, the place where God chose to manifest His presence among man. Today, God is not looking for talent, splendor, or riches. He's looking for a tattered tent, a person that has weathered the trials of life and is willing to yield themselves fully to become His dwelling place. His presence in your life will cause the talents and abilities that reside in you to flow out in an abundance of ministry, but it is His presence that will bring eternal fruit.

Many today are attempting to build ministries and legacies built on natural success. God told Moses, in Exodus 33, that he would have success, but His presence would not go with Him because the people were stiff necked. Moses pleaded for God's presence. Today, we must also become desperate for more of the presence of the Lord in our lives.

The Presence of God as seen in the Shekinah Glory above the Ark of the Covenant was restored. His Presence and Glory transformed all who worshipped at David's Tabernacle. This was altogether different from the tabernacle which

Moses had built. This was a new thing. A new order. There was rejoicing, praise, and worship. The Psalms we love so well were born at David's Tabernacle. David himself entered in to a new ministry. God's glory had been restored in the midst of His people. (Graham Truscott)

In the tabernacle of David, the glory of God was the priority. David learned through tragic trial and error — the death of cousin Uzza — that God must be consulted about every step, and that God's presence was priority. The tabernacle was more than a place to hear the modern and trendy songs. It was a place to encounter God. Songs were birthed from the place of His presence. A nation was changed because the priority was His presence! God wants to restore in you a tabernacle, a dwelling for His glory. Everything changes when His glory comes to stay, but the cost of sacrifice is well worth the reward of having Him!

Day Thirty-Nine

Hide and Seek

In that day it will be said to Jerusalem: "Do not be afraid, Zion; let not your hands be weak. "The Lord your God is in your midst, The Mighty One, will save; He will rejoice over you with gladness, He will quiet you with His love, He will rejoice over you with singing.
Zephaniah 3:16-17, NKJV

The name *Zephaniah* means "the Lord hides." He prophesied during the reign of Josiah (639-609 B.C.), who was Judah's last godly ruler. It is probable that Zephaniah's prophecies helped to inspire the reforms that Josiah made in purifying Solomon's Temple and establishing some moral order. Zephaniah prophesied concerning the coming judgment or "the great day of the Lord" about God's rebellious people. This phrase is often used to describe the end times and coming judgment.

Have you ever felt that God was hiding from you? Maybe you are facing a time now that reminds you of the childhood game "hide and seek" — only God is the one hiding. These seasons of our lives become an opportunity for editing and cleaning house. What in your life do you need to hit the "delete" button on (and never press "undo")? What area of your life do you need to move the furniture clean where the dirt has collected?

In the midst of restructuring, cleaning, and editing, God says, "Do not fear." It may seem like the hour in which we live is bleak and destruction is imminent, but *let not your hands be weak.* Why? *The Lord YOUR God in your midst, the Mighty One, will save; He will rejoice over you with gladness, He will quiet you with His love, He will rejoice over you with singing.*

God is laughing at His enemies. God is singing, dancing, laughing, and delighting Himself in your life. He knows this present struggle is making an opportunity for Him to display His glory in you. God is confident in His glory, confident that He can work on your behalf! You can have confidence in His glory also.

The Lord is trying to get His people simply to "lighten up." It is a serious delusion for us to take ourselves, or our work too seriously because that is usually an indication that we are still moving in our own human energy. The Lord really does sit in the heavens and laugh (Psalm 2:4), and when we are truly seated with Him, seeing from His perspective, we, too, will begin to laugh at many of the things we are so uptight about now. (Rick Joyner)

The Lord is purging you and cleansing you from your striving and sin. Oh, those things that have kept us from pressing into Him more. It is His desire to come and quiet your carnal stirrings and He does it by His love and songs of delight. We strive over frivolous distractions, while the Creator is singing over us with delight. We cannot hear His beautiful notes because our ears are striving to listen to the distractions and noise around us. Today, His love will clear away the noise and bring you into His joy. It is time to rest in Him.

Day Forty

Not by Might

So he answered and said to me, "This is the word of the Lord to Zerubbabel: 'Not by might nor by power, but by My Spirit,' says the Lord of hosts. Zechariah 4:6, NKJV

We are living in days in which people have grown cold to the Gospel, and church people have grown cold to prayer and passionate New Testament living. Much like the woman with the issue of blood (Luke 8), we need heavenly virtue to flow into our emaciated bodies again.

The church has found itself like this frail woman — having spent all she has, only growing worse, becoming an unclean outcast, and incapable of fulfilling her divine purpose. Playing politics, preaching a social gospel, or avoiding the hard truths of Scripture will not change the core problem. Only the power of the Holy Spirit can immediately restore strength, health, and vitality.

Today, what area of your life needs the restoration power of God? Where have you relied on man's efforts rather than the power of the Holy Spirit? Allow God to transform, revitalize, and refresh you today!

Without the Spirit's power at work, our human efforts to find freedom, build the church, and walk in discipleship — though they may be good — will have short-lived results (1 Corinthians 3:12-13). May the overflow of our Christianity be the result of continued reliance on the Holy Spirit's boundless power.

All forms of successful revival depend upon absolute reliance on God's Spirit. Zerubbabel faced huge problems in the revival of the temple and Jerusalem. The recipe for this type of revival is simple. Revival will not occur if the revivalist depends on human force, wealth, or well-trained armies. Revival will not occur based on human power, strength or the capacity simply to produce something. Revival is accomplished when those who seek to repair the broken-down temple boundaries of spirituality and trust in the operation of the Holy Spirit. (The Revival Study Bible)

Pastors, another church growth campaign is not the answer. Reviving by the Spirit of God is the only hope. Believers, the only way to a happier life is a revived first love in God. Let us return to full reliance on the Spirit's power. Let us return to the uncompromised preaching of the

Word of God in which God is fully exalted and magnified. Let us return to a priority on prayer and purity. These must come as we are awakened again by the Spirit of God, for it is here that we are truly empowered. It is here, in the preaching of the Word, that the power of God for salvation flows (Romans 1:16). It is here, in the prayer-saturated life, that power overflows in the believer (James 5:16). It is here, in purity, that power can flow freely without the blockages of sin.

It is time to rely on the power of God and not the efforts of man. Whenever the power of God is not relied upon, man will always intervene and worship a golden calf. Lord, remove the blockages and revive me today according to your Word, for it is so great a power!

Day Forty-One

Righteous Fire

But who can endure the day of His coming? And who can stand when He appears? For He is like a refiner's fire and like launderer's soap. He will sit as a refiner and purifier of silver, and He will purify the sons of Levi and purge them like gold and silver, that they may offer to the Lord an offering in righteousness. Malachi 3:2-3, NKJV

As St. Augustine said, "Therefore, we pray to God for the enablement of what He calls us to do and what He calls others to do. In fact, this is exactly why prayer is necessary. Only God can do what needs to be done. We are so sinful and so rebellious and so hard and resistant that if we are left to ourselves, we will carry on exactly as the people did in 2 Chronicles 30:10, with 'scorn and mockery.'"

In the purging process, refiners will skim the impurities from the precious metal as it is heated. This process is repeated multiple times in order to form a clean and precious result. Removing stains from laundry is very similar. The process involves scrubbing, washing, and rewashing until the stain is removed.

Paul admonishes us to offer ourselves to this cleansing process (Romans 12:1-2). Climbing on the altar of sacrifice means that our desires, lusts, cravings, and sinful nature are being consumed by the righteous fire of God. The more we are transformed, the more God's perfect will and nature begin to shine forth out of our lives.

When cleaning an old piece of furniture that has grown dirty in color, the effort of cleansing causes the original color and beauty to shine through. You would not only clean half of the piece of furniture and leave the other half to remain dirty. God thoroughly cleans us so that His nature and His desires can fully be seen in our lives. Are you offering yourself freely on the altar of worship before God, or is it a constant battle for God to sanctify you wholly? Today, what is God desiring to clean in your life?

One of the greatest mercies that you will ever have will be a revelation to your heart of how to get rid of yourself. Boundless spiritual resources are available after the flesh no longer reigns. (Smith Wigglesworth)

What great purpose and use in the Master's hand will come when self is removed? The debris that has stopped your spiritual well, once removed, will cause the well-spring of life to overflow. It is truly a continual process to keep the well clear of debris, the vine of trimmed of fruitless branches, the garment washed of sinful spots, the gold cleansed from impurities. The altar of refinement must stay lit and our lives continually applied to its fire so that we may ceaselessly be transformed into His image. Surrender today to the washing and cleansing God desires to perform in the inner parts of your life.

Day Forty-Two

Heights of the Heavenlies

Who may ascend into the hill of the Lord? Or who may stand in His holy place? He who has clean hands and a pure heart, who has not lifted up his soul to an idol and nor sworn deceitfully. He shall receive blessing from the Lord, and righteousness from the God of his salvation. This is Jacob, the generation of those who seek Him, who seek Your face. Selah
Psalm 24:3-6, NKJV

I pray that it is your desire to climb the heights of the heavenlies and ascend into the expansive mountains of the greatness of God. Growing up, my family would often take trips across the Appalachian Mountains through the Blue Ridge Parkway. Later in life, I enjoyed the Rocky Mountains, and I have driven through the Ozark Mountains. Every time, I am amazed at the splendor of God's creation. The mountaintop gives you a different perspective of the earth below. There is a different atmosphere, a different climate. Even the vegetation and wildlife on the mountains are different. So it is with the presence of God.

Are you satisfied with staying at the base of the mountain while others ascend the heights into the glory cloud around the mountaintop? Would you, like Moses and Joshua, go up to the presence of the Lord, or are you content to engage in revelry at the base of the mountain? The journey of encountering His presence on the mountain begins by examining your spiritual condition. Only those willing to pay the price to forsake the sinful carnality at the base of the mountain may ascend to the presence of God at the mountaintop. Have you begun the ascent into greater things with God or are you still indecisive about the fading pleasures down below?

When driving a vehicle, a driver must maintain focus out the front window. Occasional glances at the side mirrors show us where we have come from and ensure our safety. However, the driver's focus is not set on the side mirrors. Likewise, in our Christian walk, we must resist the temptation to become focused on "side mirror objects" that "appear closer that what they are" and maintain our focus on where God is taking us—deeper into His presence.

For months, they had waited on God. Nothing happened, until one night a young man, Bible in hand began reading from Psalm 24, "Who may ascend into the hill of the Lord? Or who may stand in His holy place? He who has clean hands and a pure heart." He shut his Bible. Looking at his companions, he said, "Brethren, it seems to me so much humbug waiting as we are...unless we are rightly related to God. I must ask myself: Are my hands clean? Is my heart pure?" He then began to pray...At that moment, something happened in the barn. A power was let loose that shook the parish from center to circumference...God had visited them, and neither they nor the parish could ever be the same again.* (The Lewis Revival)

Be cleansed and come up into His presence. Forsake the old, foolish, carnal way below, and come higher up the mountain. There you will encounter God. There you will witness Him in great power and glory. There, on the mountain peak of His glory, God will write with His finger on the tablet of your heart His indelible Word. It is in His glory you will be sanctified and be forever changed!

Day Forty-Three

God's Recipe

If My people who are called by My name will humble themselves, and pray and seek My face, and turn from their wicked ways, then I will hear from heaven, and will forgive their sin and heal their land. 2 Chronicles 7:14, NKJV

Often we try to formulate a special "recipe" that will bring about revival. Many times throughout Scripture, we find promises of God that come with prerequisites. For example, Romans 10:9: *that if you confess with your mouth the Lord Jesus and believe in your heart that God has raised Him from the dead, you will be saved.* However, we often disconnect verses like this from Ephesians 2:8-9: *For by grace you have been saved through faith, and that not of yourselves...not of works...* Ultimately, we know we are born again because the Holy Spirit has convicted us and revealed to us the truth of God's Word, which then produces faith in one's heart along with a public confession and lifestyle of salvation.

It works likewise, with revival. 2 Chronicles 7:14, is sometimes used to formulate a recipe independent of true repentance. Revival is the awakening of a person's affections towards God. It is the bringing back to life of the basic essential of our relationship with God — our first love. This awakening restores our passion for worship, our passion for the Word, our passion for evangelism, our passion for prayer, our passion for holiness, and our passion for the promises of God's Word.

God is not looking for someone to plug in a certain formula for revival: He is simply looking for those who, by the Spirit's drawing, will humble themselves and repent, and who, by repentance, will seek His face.

The Spirit of God convicts so that we might enter into refreshing by the presence of the Lord. God is working at the hearts of His people that they may return to Him through repentance and prayer so that His reviving work may be accomplished.

No one has ever manifested the power of God like the Son of God, Jesus Christ. Before He entered His public ministry, He spent time with the Father in prayer. Jesus was known to have spent seasons of prayer alone with the Father. These seasons of prayer were the source of His power. He could do nothing unless the Father revealed it to Him. (David Yonggi Cho)

God is not looking for mega churches or great orators. He is stirring the hearts of His people to humility and absolute dependence upon Him. This is where revival flows. God is looking for the one whose heart is humbled, repentant, and dependent upon Him.

Pride will keep you from living life behind the veil. Pride will keep you in dead works and outside of His awakening power. It will harden the heart and bring about destruction. Humility and repentance will avert disaster. Humility and repentance will bring the power of new life. Humility and repentance will bring you into the presence chamber of God.

Day Forty-Four

Critical Crossroads

In the year that King Uzziah died, I saw the Lord sitting on a throne, high and lifted up, and the train of His robe filled the temple.
Isaiah 6:1, NKJV

We find Isaiah at a critical crossroads. He was facing a death of leadership, and the future was uncertain. We can liken Isaiah's critical crossroads to the strategic point the Church is at today. The question that we are all faced with: Will we continue the journey in man's efforts with a non-offensive, social gospel, or will we take up the journey of the uncompromising and loving Word of God. When we allow unrighteousness to die, we can truly see the Lord in all His splendor.

The compromised, self-centered, social gospel message will not transform our world. We must see the Lord sitting on His throne. We must experience the tangible presence and power of an Almighty God. The message of the Gospel descriptively addresses the root of all racial divide, the origins of the violence of man, the selfishness and depravity of the human race. The Gospel addresses the wars and rumors of wars to come. The Word of God depicts the diseases and pestilence we are facing in our generation. The solution is not better politics. The solution is not a watered-down poem from the pulpit. The solution is a transformed heart and mind by the power of the Holy Spirit and the Word of God.

Individually, we must return to the fear of God by seeing Him where He is seated — as Isaiah saw Him in the midst of a perverse generation — on His throne. Then we begin to recognize that the depravity of man truly begins within ourselves individually. We recognize we are all undone and in need of God. We fully recognize our need when we come face to face with Him in His majesty.

Before a sinful man can think a right thought of God, there must have been a work of enlightenment done within him; imperfect it may be, but a true work nonetheless, and the secret cause of all desiring and seeking and praying which may follow. We pursue God because, and only because, He has first put an urge within us that spurs us to the pursuit. (A.W. Tozer, 1897-1963)

How do you respond when royalty comes in the room? When the absolute Sovereign of the universe sits down before you, you become aware of your inadequacies and how wonderful and perfect He is. When

God's glory fills His temple, you are drawn in to His beauty and captivated by His presence. When He speaks, nothing else matters. When God walks into the room, you simply do not want to miss out on anything about Him. Like a child, you want to be as close as you can, but with great awe and fear you wonder how close you can get and still survive.

We need God to take His throne in our lives and churches again. The reign of man's control must come to an end. Death to self is the only option if we desire to see God in His glory as Isaiah did the year King Uzziah died.

Day Forty-Five

Praise is the Plow

Sow for yourselves righteousness; reap in mercy; break up your fallow ground, for it is time to seek the Lord, 'till He comes and rains righteousness on you.
Hosea 10:12, NKJV

Fallow ground is ground that has been plowed and made ready for seed sowing; however, it has not been maintained nor has seed been sown. The result is hard clumps of clay that cannot be useful until it is plowed again and made ready to receive seed.

In Hosea 10:11, the prophet says, "Judah shall plow." *Judah* means "praise." The picture that has been displayed, is that our praise becomes the instrument to soften the hardened heart and prepare it for seeds of righteousness. Praise prepares the soil of your life to receive the seed of God's Word — His righteousness — by faith, which produces a harvest of mercy. The righteousness of God comes also in the form of rain. God supplies seed for our soil and ensures the harvest will come in due season. We must be willing to praise and receive from Heaven.

God will plant His Word in our hearts and even ensure the nutrients to nourish that seed are provided. We must remain open and receptive to all that God has for us. Spiritual vitality and fruitfulness are the result of learning to rest and receive from God.

Praise confronts the indifference of a fallow, spiritually cold heart. Revival fully embraces the plow of praise and prepares the heart to pursue God. Revival causes us to dig deep into the soil of our lives to ensure the ground is fully prepared to receive all that God has for us. The harvest is proportional to how we prepare and yield to God.

Now again, the shadow of darkness and death is over this generation like nothing we have ever had before. And yet, the greatest tragedy of all is this: a sick Church in a dying world. We have neither the vision nor the passion, nor at this moment, the intention of setting our house in order — to break the fallow ground — to prepare the way of the Lord. My hope is that as we go on from here, we are not just going to gather information and statistics about revival, but that individually, we are going to seek personal revival." (Leonard Ravenhill)

Personal revival at its essence is a full returning of our hearts, lives, emotions, affections, desires, will — our whole person — to Christ. Praise of Him becomes paramount in our lives. Utter dependence upon God for sustaining life and power is our driver. The fruitfulness of our praise is godly character and power which in turn becomes ministry to others.

Oftentimes, we busy ourselves with attempting to break up the fallow ground in others, when yet our hearts are still hardened to His presence. We become burnt out, exhausted, and depleted of joy as we suffer the physical effects of not having a heart that is overflowing with personal awakening. Determine to have the fallow ground of your heart softened today as you humble yourself before God. Praise Him in a way He is deserving of and watch the fruit of your life begin to sweeten the lives of those around you.

Day Forty-Six

Give Me Children!

Now when Rachel saw that she bore Jacob no children, Rachel envied her sister, and said to Jacob, "Give me children, or else I die!"
Genesis 30:1, NKJV

How desperate are you for revival? How hungry are you for His presence? When was the last time you cried out to God with a passionate plea for more of Him? How moved with compassion are you to see the lost saved?

In this Scripture, we find that Rachel is barren. Rachel watches as her sister Leah has children, but yet Rachel has none. We can compare Rachel to Hannah. Hannah was also was unable to have children. She came before God and was moved with such desperation that, as she prayed, her lips moved, but no sound came out. The priest thought Hannah was drunk, but she was only desperate.

In Rachel's desperation, she cries out to Jacob, "Give me children, or else I die!" She was so grief stricken over her barrenness that she looked to her husband for a miracle that only God could provide.

Have we been lulled to sleep and passively go through life with no urgency or desperation to produce spiritual fruit? As Christians, we are created to reproduce spiritual babies and nurture them into mature adulthood. Do you have a desperation that God might heal your spiritual womb and produce spiritual babies from your life? Do you long for spiritual children? Give me souls, Lord, lest I die!

Revival is not a luxury, but a necessity for the nation; not an alternative but an imperative. The main reason we do not have a national revival beginning with personal revival, is that we are content to live without it. (Leonard Ravenhill)

May the Lord grant to us a genuine hunger and desperation for Him! *Blessed are those who hunger and thirst for righteousness, for they shall be filled* (Matthew 5:6, NKJV). It is a blessing to be granted such a hunger birthed by the Spirit of God. It is a blessing to know the difference between starvation that leads to death and a hungry desperation that leads to a satisfying feast. It is a blessing to be filled, not with earthly delicacies, but to feast at the table of the Lord full of spiritual delights. It is a blessing to be promised such a hope in Christ--that He should not only grant a hunger and give an understanding to us that we are spiritually hungry above any natural hunger, but that He also takes notice of those who are lowly and starving for satisfaction that only He can bring. He then humbles himself to the poorest, nastiest, most wretched of all sinners and beggars and feeds them with heavenly joys of which no tongue can fully describe. How blessed are those who hunger and thirst for righteousness!

Desperation for God always is noticed by Him. If you lack a healthy appetite for more of Him and the fruit He produces, then ask of Him who will joyfully stir in your spiritual belly a longing for something more!

Day Forty-Seven

Act According to The Word

So you shall serve the LORD your God, and He will bless your bread and your water. And I will take sickness away from the midst of you. No one shall suffer miscarriage or be barren in your land; I will fulfill the number of your days. Exodus 23:25-26, NKJV

God promises healing and restoration. He promises provision. Many today have become enamored with a prosperity message — with name-it-claim-it and positive confessions. As much as I believe in the miraculous and provision of God along with a generous lifestyle of giving, I also believe it is improper for us to abuse others for the sake of getting rich.

That being said, as Christians we have the privilege of standing steadfastly on the promises of God. We are not to misuse Scripture but are to receive all that it says God has provided. Healing, supply, wisdom, direction — all can be found in the promised supply of God.

The question is: Are you receiving, and are you expecting? We often become more aware of and more content with the report of worldly influences rather than the Word of God. Has it become easier for you to stand on what the natural man perceives, or are you holding fast to the Word of God?

Holding fast to the Word of God means taking action. We act through prayer. We act by striving to enter God's rest. We act through our praise. We act through remaining faithful stewards. We act by receiving from God. Our action is not to make or create the end result.

One final question: no matter the result, are you still taking God's Word into action? Today, what are you trusting God for? Have you acted according to the Word of God, or are you busy about making the end result happen?

Understand that there are difficulties which cannot impair prosperity, and that there is a prosperity which dominates over all external circumstances. It seems hardly correct to assert that Joseph was a prosperous man when he was to all intents and purposes in bondage. He was the property of another. Not one hour of his time belonged to himself. He was cut off from his father and from his brethren. Yet, it is distinctly stated that, notwithstanding these things, the Lord was with him and he was prosperous. (Rev. Joseph Parker)

97

Like Joseph, our dungeons may not be the result we are looking for, but it is very much God's plan. It is in the dungeon we learn to truly be free and rest in God's power. Did Joseph stay there forever? No. Did God prosper Joseph in the midst of his enemies? Yes!

God had given Joseph a dream—a word! Likewise, God has given us His Word. He is truly faithful to complete the work which He has begun. Keep walking according to what He has spoken. Do not turn from His Word for its promises are not empty.

Day Forty-Eight

No Fear

And he said, "Listen, all you of Judah and you inhabitants of Jerusalem, and you, King Jehoshaphat! Thus says the LORD to you: 'Do not be afraid nor dismayed because of this great multitude, for the battle is not yours, but God's. Tomorrow go down against them. They will surely come up by the Ascent of Ziz, and you will find them at the end of the brook before the Wilderness of Jeruel. You will not need to fight in this battle. Position yourselves, stand still and see the salvation of the Lord, who is with you, O Judah and Jerusalem!' Do not fear or be dismayed; tomorrow go out against them, for the Lord is with you."

And Jehoshaphat bowed his head with his face to the ground, and all Judah and the inhabitants of Jerusalem bowed before the Lord, worshiping the Lord. Then the Levites of the children of the Kohathites and of the children of the Korahites stood up to praise the Lord God of Israel with voices loud and high.
2 Chronicles 20:15-19, NKJV

Have you ever found yourself fearful of what you might say to someone — how to share your God story? Maybe you have written off personal evangelism in your life and designated that as the "pastor's job".

We must move forward as believers with the assurance that as we face our opposition, the sound of our praise and the declaration of God's Word will penetrate the hearts of the enemy, rendering them completely incapacitated by grace.

Too many times, we think the battle of salvation is our fight and that somehow our cunning words will win the war over someone's soul. Remember, victory is the Lord's! Salvation is the result of grace on someone's heart. Our job is to stand steadfastly on God's Word and His praise, and then see the miraculous victory of God. It is time to position yourself in praise.

As you watch God melt the hardened heart, transform the critic, and overcome the belligerent, you will recognize your position is to remain unwavering in your passion for God and allow His grace to affect those you minister to. Engage in personal evangelism, for it is there you will carry off the spoils of war brought to you by God.

Preaching salvation must be more than a cold-water business. Conversions are produced in the fire. Evangelism is not a clinical operation; it is a hot affair. Conversion must be of the Spirit. This is not a business transaction. Holy Spirit preaching makes Holy Spirit converts, not technical converts, or theological converts. We believe with the heart. The answer for this nation is not polemics and debate, but the consistent, bright-burning witness of genuine believers. Let me remind you, if you want to be rid of the darkness, stop arguing and just switch on the light!" (Reinhard Bonnke)

The light of God's glory is radiating in you today. It is time to worship Him with the sounds of thanksgiving and telling the story of God's great mercy. As you sing the song of redemption that God has given you, His mercy will surely affect the lives of those around you.

Day Forty-Nine

Too Great a Work

So I sent messengers to them, saying, "I am doing a great work, so that I cannot come down. Why should the work cease while I leave it and go down to you?"
Nehemiah 6:3, NKJV

We are busy about the Kingdom work of rebuilding broken down lives. We are snatching souls from the burning heaps of rubble all the while, facing threats, assaults, obstacles, and distractions from those who oppose the work of God.

Imagine for a moment that Nehemiah had come down from the wall, distracted by the taunts of those who were after him in the "Valley of *Oh-No.*" His work would have ceased, others would have lapsed in their labors, and at most, the work would have mustered a half-hearted investment upon their return to labor. As we pursue God, it is imperative to stay out of the "Valley of *Oh-No.*" Do not stop being faithful. Do not stop your passionate prayers. Many will come to distract you and assault you along the journey. Keep your hand to the task God has placed before you.

The scope of the project should not worry you. God is both the author and the finisher of the work He has begun in you (Hebrews 12:2). Remain steadfast and enjoy the completion of the rebuilt walls, the lives God restores, around you.

What work is God establishing in and through your life? Be encouraged. God's success is not dependent upon your insecurities, your fears, your doubts, or the taunts and ridicules of others. God is full in control, and as you yield to His plan today, you will find yourself "about too great a work" to come off the walls of restoration.

Hence the answer of Nehemiah to each attack; he refuses to discuss, meet, plead his cause, justify his motives, or defend his actions or the work. He answers each renewed attack the same way. He will not back down. He will not give up. He will not assume there is truth to what they are saying even though what they say at a surface level may appear so; he will not give in to fear because of peer pressure, political or even artificial prophetic opposition, or intimidation. He knows he is a servant of both the Lord and the people. He knows he has a job to do for the Lord, that is great and large, and the people who are to be involved have to be brought to a unity of accomplishment in God where previously they have been shamed, separated, and scattered. He was indeed a man sent from God. (William Pratney)

The work of the Lord in you is a great work. The work of the Lord through you in the lives of others is a great work. Eternity is hanging in the balance. Let us consider Christ the captain of our salvation and follow closely to Him as the work endures. He has certainly given the command, He has given us the Holy Spirit's power, and we are yielded to the fulfillment of the plan of Heaven. There is coming a day and an hour when the enemies of the cross will be fully subdued. Until then, march on! There is still too great a work both in you personally and in the lives of those around you that must be carried on.

Day Fifty

Harvest of Joy

Then our mouth was filled with laughter, and our tongue with singing. Then they said among the nations, "The Lord has done great things for them." The Lord has done great things for us, and we are glad.
Psalm 126:2-3, NKJV

I will never forget the first time I experienced the supernatural joy of the Lord. I found myself laughing with great joy for what seemed like hours and was completely overcome for months by this refreshing joy of the Lord. Today, I am still thankful for this joy of the Lord within me. I still find myself often overcome with His joy and delight.

Scripture is full of testimony of this supernatural joy and a life of joy in God. According to John 15, our greatest joy is found in our pursuit of God and the fruitfulness this pursuit brings. The fruitful Christian life can be found in the overflow of ministry to others. The quality of this fruit is determined by our character and how we display the fruit of the Spirit. But each Christian ought to reproduce spiritual fruit of ministry to others. Could it be that lack of joy in your life is directly related to the lack of receiving seed from God and sowing that seed in the lives of others?

In the example of the vine and the branches from John 15, we are the branches and Christ is the vine. The "overflow" or fruit of our vines is godly character and ministry. The quality of the fruit is determined by how we yield to the work of God in the transformation of our character.

Today, ask God to mature your fruit. Allow Him to change your character and produce in you spiritual fruit. Allow God to increase your ability to bear much fruit in ministry to others. Lord, give us fruit that remains! As you sow your seeds in ministry to others, know that God is bringing forth a harvest of joy in your life!

Perhaps if there were more of that intense distress for souls that leads to tears, we should more frequently see the results we desire. Sometimes it may be that while we are complaining of the hardness of the hearts of those we are seeking to benefit, the hardness of our own hearts and our feeble apprehension of the solemn reality of eternal things may be the true cause of our lack of success.
(James Hudson Taylor)

Those who sow in tears shall reap in joy. He who continually goes forth weeping, bearing seed for sowing, shall doubtless come again with rejoicing, bringing his sheaves with him (Psalm 126:5-6, NKJV). God is giving you a harvest of joy! Where you have sown in uncertainty, trusting the promises of God, you will reap in joy! Where you have asked of Him to mature your fruitfulness and that process of transformation has been through test and trial, know that in your harvest comes fullness of joy.

You can experience His supernatural joy overflowing in your life today. His joy is more than a concept or idea. t is a reality that can overtake you and bring you strength. His joy is your strength (Nehemiah 8:10)!

Day Fifty-One

Flames of Fire

And Jesus went about all Galilee, teaching in their synagogues, preaching the gospel of the kingdom, and healing all kinds of sickness and all kinds of disease among the people. Then His fame went throughout all Syria; and they brought to Him all sick people who were afflicted with various diseases and torments, and those who were demon-possessed, epileptics, and paralytics; and He healed them. Great multitudes followed Him – from Galilee, and from Decapolis, Jerusalem, Judea, and beyond the Jordan.
Matthew 4:23-25, NKJV

God makes His ministers a flame of fire (Hebrews 1:7). Jesus went throughout the countryside, towns, and villages as a burning and shining light of hope and healing to all who would receive Him. His message was a burning fire of righteousness. His ministry was fire consuming sickness and disease. The fame of Jesus spread like wildfire. And the multitudes who followed Christ were touched by the fire of God.

This passage of Scripture gives a wonderful picture of what happens when hearts are awakened to the ministry of Christ. The hurting and the broken come. Multitudes are hungry for one moment in His presence.

May God prepare in us a place for the multitudes to receive this all-consuming fire personally. May we travail in prayer that even one soul might be snatched from the flames of hell to be set ablaze in a passionate pursuit of God.

Have you been touched by the fire of God? Is there a passionate, all-consuming fire from God burning in your soul? Like on the Day of Pentecost, there is a flame of fire for you to receive, and it will so ignite your soul that no earthly passion would compare. Fan into flame today your fire (2 Timothy 1:6). Let the passion of your first love be reignited. This world is tired of smoldering church embers and is in desperate need for a Pentecostal flame of fire.

Their preaching mainly turns on the important points of humanity's guilt, corruption, and impotence. They equally stress supernatural regeneration by the Spirit of God and free justification by faith in the righteousness of Christ and the new birth. Their preaching is not with the enticing words of man's wisdom. Rather, they speak wisdom among them that are perfect. Burning love for Christ and souls warms their breasts and energizes their work. In most places where they labor, God has clearly worked with them and confirmed the Word by signs following. (William Cooper)

Our generation needs the fire of God today! His fire will purify, bring power, and light the path ahead. Jeremiah described this fire of God's word burning in his bones (Jeremiah 20:9). The fire of God will transform you, and others will be affected by the flames that burn in you.

Day Fifty-Two

The Father's Blessing

Ask, and it will be given to you; seek, and you will find; knock, and it will be opened to you. For everyone who asks receives, and he who seeks finds, and to him who knocks it will be opened. Or what man is there among you who, if his son asks for bread, will give him a stone? Or if he asks for a fish, will he give him a serpent? If you then, being evil, know how to give good gifts to your children, how much more will your Father who is in heaven give good things to those who ask Him! Therefore, whatever you want men to do to you, do also to them, for this is the Law and the Prophets.
Matthew 7:7-12, NKJV

The Toronto Outpouring in 1994, became known as "The Father's Blessing" because of the awareness of the Father's love in the meetings and those ministered to at the revival. Throughout the revival, emphasis was placed on learning to "soak" in or receive God's love.

It is true that each of us must learn to saturate ourselves over and over again in the love of God. We know that according to Matthew 7:11, it is our Heavenly Father's desire to give us good gifts, and the very best gift He gave was Himself.

Paul taught us in his letter to the Galatians that the Holy Spirit helps us understand our Father's love and even cries out "Abba, Father" (Galatians 4:6). The love of God is more than a concept. God is love (1 John 4:8). This is more than an adjective. Love in this context is a noun. Love is not only describing the character of God, but love is who God is. The Father's love cannot be contained within our human experience. It is an eternal, unstoppable love. It cannot be likened to any earthly person's love. This love is unique and can be experienced personally.

Have you rested in the love of God lately? Are you saturating yourself in God's love through worship, through reading His Word, through soaking in His presence? Today, persistently step into this endless fountain of love.

Too often, we knock at mercy's door and then run away, instead of waiting for an entrance and an answer. We act as if we were afraid of having our prayers answered. A great many people pray in that way; they do not wait for the answer. Our Lord teaches us here that we are not only to ask, but we are to wait for the answer; if it does not come, we must seek to find out the reason. We are to ask with a beggar's humility, to seek with a servant's carefulness, and to knock with the confidence of a friend. (D.L. Moody)

Your Heavenly Father has good and perfect gifts to bestow liberally upon His children. It is His desire to lavish His blessings upon you in greater ways you have yet to know. Our Father knows what we need before we ask (Matthew 6:8), and He has this foreknowledge of our needs because He alone is God. God is all-knowing and thus He knows and cares for everything about us. He knows our needs and calls us boldly before His throne because He is our creator. The One who formed us from the dust of the ground knows our frame and considers our needs. He knows our need because He is our Father, so, He understands our needs greater than any earthly father, and He cares for us and supplies for our needs greater than any earthly father. He knows our needs before we ask, and He hears of them when we ask. We can come with assurance before our God and rest in His great love. Bask in His presence and know that whatever you bring before Him, He hears, He knows, He understands, and He answers!

Day Fifty-Three

Prepare for the Miraculous

But Jesus looked at them and said, "With men it is impossible, but not with God; for with God all things are possible." Then Peter began to say to Him, "See, we have left all and followed You."
Mark 10:27-28, NKJV

God is working miracles on your behalf! In this moment, He is working all around you! An awakening to the presence and the work of God is happening all around us. An awareness that God is desiring to work not just around but through us requires that we prepare to engage in this work.

It is quite possible that two teenagers might be physically capable of having a baby. However, does this ensure that these two are adequately prepared to nurture and parent this child? We know that raising a child in a healthy environment requires finances, mental and emotional support, a community of family and friends, and much more. Likewise, even as we would prepare for a newborn, we must also be prepared for spiritual newborns.

Like Peter, can we say that we have left all to follow Christ (Matthew 19:27)? Have we made room for the miraculous? Have we prepared ourselves to engage wholly in ministry to others? If you are willing to lay your life in the hands of Jesus, you will find that He will fully and adequately supply you with all resources necessary to minister to the spiritual newborns. Are you willing to lay down your life today so that you can find new life in service to others through Christ (Matthew 16:25)?

If you're going to have a houseguest, you adjust your lifestyle to accommodate him. You prepare a room for her to sleep in, maybe putting the kids together in one room. You set another place at mealtime. You modify what you wear around the house. The list goes on. Just as you prepare for a visit from your friend, you must also prepare for a visitation from The Friend. True revival will change you and your church – forever! (Steve Hill)

Making room for revival in your life means that humility and repentance must have its full work in you. Humility and repentance before God will cause priorities to change, attitudes to be adjusted, and availability to the work of God to increase. Repentance clears out dead works and religious mindsets. Repentance places a demand on the regenerating, reviving, resuscitating power of God. Humility acknowledges weakness and leans into the perfecter. Humility breaks open the hardness and causes repentance to flow out.

Here the house is prepared. It is in humility and repentance that the foundation for revival is laid and the house is built. Through them, the life of revival is sustained. Genuine revival will overflow from genuine people who humble themselves and live a repentant life. God is always welcome in a home that has prepared itself and maintains itself in humility and repentance.

Day Fifty-Four

Now is the Time

And as you go, preach, saying, "The kingdom of heaven is at hand.' Heal the sick, cleanse the lepers, raise the dead, cast out demons. Freely you have received, freely give.
Matthew 10:7-8, NKJV

In this Scripture we find Jesus commissioning His disciples to be sent out for ministry. Their message was clear — the Kingdom of Heaven. The power for ministry was made available. Today, the same is true. Our message is the Kingdom of Heaven and all power for this ministry has been made available.

The message of the Kingdom is the message of Christ, beginning with salvation by grace through faith. The power for ministry confirms the Word of God and shows God's compassion for others. Paul explained to the Corinthian believers regarding his message that it was of the Spirit's demonstration of power so that faith might be in God, not man (1 Corinthians 2:4-5).

Have you received healing in your body? Has God delivered you from addiction? What have you received from Christ? The power of God that was made available to you in these areas of your life becomes the place from where His power flows to minister to others. Your victory is your sermon! Your testimony is your platform! Share your God story, and use Scripture to show this love of God that transforms lives. Allow God's power to confirm His Word in and through you. This testimony impacts the hearers and releases overcoming power in your life (Revelation 12:11).

The disciples had experienced personal ministry from Jesus. They watched as He ministered to and taught others. Every ounce of power needed to fulfill this commission was available to them. Now was their time. Likewise, you have received from God. You have watched His ministry to others. Every ounce of power needed has been made available to you. Boldness has been provided through the Holy Spirit. Trust the Holy Spirit who is teaching you (1 John 2:27). Now is the time!

When you have the Holy Ghost, you have an empire, a power within yourself. (William J. Seymour)

The understanding here is that you are not only "going," but you are being "sent." Christ has commissioned you and sent you out as His minister. His message is clear: the kingdom of heaven is at hand and the only way to obtain this kingdom is through repentance in Christ. The authority to proclaim this message has been extended to you, and the ability to confirm this message with sign and wonders is made available. The motivation for this ministry is that you have freely received of His ministry, and the ability to share it with others is to freely give. It is without reservation or price that we extend the message of the Gospel and its power to salvation. Today is the day of salvation. Now is the time!

Day Fifty-Five

The Spirit of Truth

However, when He, the Spirit of truth, has come, He will guide you into all truth; for He will not speak on His own authority, but whatever He hears He will speak; and He will tell you things to come. He will glorify Me, for He will take of what is Mine and declare it to you. All things that the Father has are Mine. Therefore, I said that He will take of Mine and declare it to you.
John 16:13-15, NKJV

Jesus said in John 14:6, He is *the way, the truth and the life.* Thus, the Holy Spirit, who is Christ's representative will speak only of the truth in Christ. Here in John 16, Jesus further explains that the Holy Spirit will glorify Him (Christ). It is clear by Jesus' teaching that the Holy Spirit—the Spirit of Truth—reveals to us the truth and teaching of Christ. In John 1:14, John said that the Word of God was made flesh and dwelt among us. Christ is the expressed image of God's Word, and the Holy Spirit reveals Jesus to us.

Further, Jesus explains that the Holy Spirit will reveal all that belongs to the Father. Jesus wants us to live a full, abundant, and overflowing Christian life. He wants us to know all that is available to us as believers. Jesus said He came for us to have abundant life (John 10:10). Paul taught us that every spiritual blessing has been made available to us (Ephesians 1:3). Are you receiving from the Holy Spirit all the truth, direction, and resources available?

As Ephesians 3:20 says, there is *exceedingly abundantly above all that we can ask or think"* available. We need the power of the Holy Spirit operating in our lives to receive all the fullness available to us.

When the Spirit comes into believers, He comes to tell them all about Jesus' salvation. He reveals Christ. He paints Him as the wonderful Son of God, the brightest gem the Father had in heaven – our only hope of salvation and reconciliation with the Father. How sweet it is to have the Holy Ghost come to you and show you Jesus through the Word. He witnesses and reveals through the Word and never gets outside of the Word. Speak through me, Holy Spirit, with a tongue of praise for Jesus, and still all criticism and harsh talk. Amen.
(William J. Seymour)

The Holy Spirit, the Spirit of truth, the Spirit of reality, has come. He is illuminating the Word. He is glorifying Christ. He is taking the exact imprint of the Father, which is the Son, and He is making Him a reality to us. He is making His promises a reality to us. He is making His heavenly kingdom a reality to us. He is making His power a reality to us. This is more than emotionalism or a good service. He is more than a feeling we get when a guest minister preaches. The Spirit of reality is illuminating our heart, our emotions, our mind, our will, our affections — our whole being — to the reality of experience in Christ. To read in Scripture that God is love is of itself a powerful truth, but how much more real, personal, and intimate does that love become as the Spirit of reality brings us into that love. Our emotions are stirred, our hearts are longing, our minds are illuminated, our logic is heightened, our desires change, and our will is melted. When the reality of His love floods our heart, it is no more just a truth in His Word, it is my truth written on my heart, enriching my emotions, stimulating my mind, and directing the course of my life. The Spirit of reality wants to make every part of Christ real to you.

Day Fifty-Six

Abide in Christ

"I am the vine, you are the branches. He who abides in Me, and I in him, bears much fruit; for without Me you can do nothing.
John 15:5, NKJV

John 15 is a wonderful passage of discipleship, the joy of our pursuit in God, and the power of God available to those who rely upon God. Christ makes His point clear: true and effective religion is useless without abiding. Abiding in Christ is the source of all true affections towards God; without this, we merely are left with man's efforts and attempts to please God. The description in the Greek would be that we are to remain in Christ. Here are some matters of abiding we must assess in our life.

Closely related to abiding is that of continuing. This would suggest that we are to remain steadfastly secure in Christ. Colossians 1:21-23 states that we have been reconciled to God and are to be presented blameless at His coming, with the condition *if indeed you continue in the faith, grounded and steadfast, and are not moved away from the hope of the gospel.*

A further step in this journey of abiding would be enduring. There are many ups and downs in our journey with Christ. Paul told Timothy in 2 Timothy 2:10 that he "endured all things for the sake of the elect." Verse 12 of the same passage states that, *if we endure, we shall also reign with Him.*

It is also important that we make firm or confirm our relationship with Christ. In 2 Peter 1:10, we are encouraged to be *diligent to make your call and election sure.* The Greek is to make it firm.

Lastly, it is necessary for us to remain faithful to the end. We know of God's faithfulness, and we are to remain faithful also. Revelation 2:10: *Be faithful until death, and I will give you the crown of life.*

The promise of eternal life made by God is sure. But abiding in the truth of the gospel, and thereby in Christ and the Father, is necessary for that life to be fulfilled. (J. Rodman Williams)

It can be the natural tendency of our flesh to cease our effort to abide and strive to earn or seek approval. The focus of being found in Christ changes to so many other distractions, even things that outwardly look "spiritual." We can begin operating in our own strength, with our own goals, and soon we our withered up, fruitless branches operating apart from Christ while quite possibly doing "good" things.

Our priority is to remain in Him, and from Him and through Him all our works flow out. We cease our self-centered striving, and we labor to be found firm and resting in Him. As we cease our labors of self-effort, then the true work of God can fully be engaged. Lord, let us draw closer to you today!

Day Fifty-Seven

Promise of the Father

And being assembled together with them, He commanded them not to depart from Jerusalem, but to wait for the Promise of the Father, "which," He said, "you have heard from Me;'
Acts 1:4, NKJV

Twice it is recorded in Luke that Jesus instructed His disciples not to leave Jerusalem but to *wait for the Promise of the Father* (Luke 24:49, Acts 1:4). It was clear the ministry, the teaching, and the impartation they had received to this point was only the beginning, and more was to come as they waited for the Promise. The disciples had waited for the Messiah to come. They had been told by the Promised One, that He was leaving, but it was advantageous for them so that another Promise of the Father may come. Today, the urgency for the power of the Holy Spirit is just as important.

There are three prevailing thoughts towards the Baptism in the Holy Spirit today. Two movements from the early twentieth century affect these beliefs. The best known is the Azusa Street Revival in 1906. Pentecostals owe great honor to those who plowed the ground at Azusa Street for the teaching on the Baptism in the Holy Spirit. This teaching is that the Baptism in the Holy Spirit is connected to speaking in tongues. The second view comes from the Holiness Movement that produced the Church of the Nazarene in 1908. This movement was birthed from the Wesleyan perfectionism, which taught that sanctification was the result of the Baptism in the Holy Spirit and had nothing to do with the "tongues movement". The third view of the Baptism in the Holy Spirit is largely influenced by the Reformed doctrine that every believer unconsciously receives the Baptism in the Holy Spirit at conversion. Both the Pentecostal Movement and the Nazarene Movement taught the Baptism in the Holy Spirit was a conscious event that was subsequent to salvation.

Today, we can experience the wonderful Baptism in the Holy Spirit. As Jesus said, wait for the Promise of the Father. It is imperative that you receive the fullness of the Holy Spirit for supernatural boldness and supernatural ministry.

If we function according to our ability alone, we get the glory; if we function according to the power of the Holy Spirit within us, God gets the glory. (Henry

T. Blackaby)

Consider the multitude of promises in Scripture concerning your life: Promises for healing, deliverance and freedom. Here we find the only promise that Jesus calls, "the Promise of the Father." This was the eternal promise that would come as a result of this new covenant of redemption. Christ would immerse His people into the very tangible presence of God in the Holy Spirit. The life of the fullness of God's Promise of the Holy Spirit is a life yielded to and reliant upon the Spirit of God. It is a life that self is buried and a power-filled life in the Spirit can exist. It is a life of divine fellowship and intimate communication with God, uninhibited by the natural barriers of flesh. Life lived in the Promise of the Father brings true order, creativity, and a reality of the heavenly world all around us. This promise is for you (Acts 2:39).

Day Fifty-Eight

The Church of Acts

And they continued steadfastly in the apostles' doctrine and fellowship, in the breaking of bread, and in prayers. Then fear came upon every soul, and many wonders and signs were done through the apostles. Now all who believed were together, and had all things in common, and sold their possessions and goods, and divided them among all, as anyone had need. So continuing daily with one accord in the temple, and breaking bread from house to house, they ate their food with gladness and simplicity of heart, praising God and having favor with all the people. And the Lord added to the church daily those who were being saved.
Acts 2:42-47, NKJV

Is the fire and fervor of the early Church revealed in the book of Acts for the Church today? We believe it is. It is important to remember that the Church in Acts was a church on fire, a church that was overflowing in power and ministry. As we find in this passage, the followers of Christ were moving together in the same direction.

When you move from one house to the next, some items get left behind. You begin to take inventory of your belongings and determine what needs to be cleared out to make room for the new. Likewise, the church of the New Testament had many leave and shipwreck their faith, but thousands of lives were added.

Together the followers of Christ ate and fellowshipped, they prayed together according to the teaching they were receiving, and they were in unity in all aspects. The disciples were faithfully meeting together at the church and privately in their homes. They maintained regular times of prayer and even called special prayer meetings. *And the Lord added to the church daily those who were being saved.*

Notice their commitment. Notice their passion. Notice the overflow from their lives. Christianity as in the Church of Acts is not passively or idly conducting religious duties, rather aggressively growing and advancing together the message of salvation and the fullness of all that God has made available.

Are the things you are living for worth Christ dying for? (Leonard Ravenhill)

Life can become cluttered with unnecessary boxes full of past successes and trophies; garments of sin we should not be wearing but we keep around for comfort; yearbooks that remind of us milestones we missed; and empty boxes we did not know we had. When awakened to our first love, we realize the clutter has been stockpiled, and it is affecting our intimacy with Christ. The old has to go, and we must become diligent in seeking Him. Passion for Christ will require the cobwebs be wiped away, and the boxes stuffed away in the corners of your heart to be revealed. He is making room for you to have more of His presence in your life. He is making room for more of His blessing in your life. He is making room for His community in your life.

Day Fifty-Nine

A House for God

Then all the multitude kept silent and listened to Barnabas and Paul declaring how many miracles and wonders God had worked through them among the Gentiles. And after they had become silent, James answered, saying, "Men and brethren, listen to me: Simon has declared how God at the first visited the Gentiles to take out of them a people for His name. And with this the words of the prophets agree, just as it is written: "After this I will return and will rebuild the tabernacle of David, which has fallen down; I will rebuild its ruins, and I will set it up; so that the rest of mankind may seek the Lord, even all the Gentiles who are called by My name, says the Lord who does all these things.'
Acts 15:12-17, NKJV

In Acts 15, we find the account of the Jerusalem Council. The council convened in about 50 AD to determine how to disciple the influx of Gentile converts. This discussion created quite a debate.

Peter and Barnabas gave accounts of the Gentiles being converted to Christ, the miracles, the Baptisms in the Holy Spirit, and so forth. After hearing all of the testimony and considering the information, the crowd grew silent.

James then prophesied from Amos 9 regarding the ministry to the Gentiles, that God was rebuilding the tabernacle of David. This prophecy is being fulfilled even in our day. God is establishing a local church, a place of worship and prayer where mankind may encounter the presence of God and know Him.

We are being built as living stones into a spiritual house, a dwelling place for God (1 Peter 2:5). In these days, God is manifesting His presence in His people and His Church. We are a living tabernacle of the glory of God. May it be your desire that His glory will increase in your life and that others would receive of His fullness.

God said He would rebuild the tabernacle of David, the only house God ever said He wanted to restore — not Moses' in its originality; not Solomon's in its splendor; but David's with its unveiled worship. It is as if what is important to God is that there are no barriers between Himself and His people. What He wants to restore is open worship of His glory; where pagans and heathens would stand outside of the circle of worshipers of David's tabernacle and see the blue flame of the shekinah glory of God between the dancing feet and the outstretched arms of twenty-four-hours-a-day, seven-days-a-week worshipers. (Tommy Tenney)

The restoring work of God prophesied by James was being applied to the Gentile ministry, but it also applies to the restoring work of God individually. Individually we are temples of the Holy Spirit (1 Corinthians 6:19). We are place where God's glory can dwell and uninhibited worship and prayer can exist. David's tabernacle was a tattered tent, but it was where the Ark of the Covenant was. It was the place of God's presence. It was also a place where perpetual worship and prayer continued daily. God is restoring His church and is restoring individuals to be tabernacles of perpetual praise and prayer where His glory can dwell.

Day Sixty

Turned Upside Down

But when they did not find them, they dragged Jason and some brethren to the rulers of the city, crying out, "These who have turned the world upside down have come here too."
Acts 17:6, NKJV

What a testimony! Those who have turned the world upside down have come here also. Paul was preaching and ministering with supernatural ministry. Multitudes came and followed him, even a great number of influential women (Acts 17:4). Those who became disgruntled began to stir a crowd to riots and violence. And in the midst of the turmoil the rulers, who incited the riots, began to shout out: *Those who have turned the world upside down have come here too.*

What do you do when others persecute you? How do you respond when those you are ministering to turn on you and incite violence against you?

David was faced with such a decision. Saul, the man he was serving, the man anointed by God, turned on him and tried to kill him. This surpasses a "bad day." The leader you respect and honor is after your life.

Interesting that Paul and Silas, in Acts 17, went to Berea to get away from the violence, and those who hated them followed them there, inciting crowds and riots in Berea. Leaving Berea, Paul went on to Athens where He preached of Jesus, the "unknown God."

The message of the Gospel brings peace to those willing to receive but divides soul and spirit (Hebrews 4:12). It gloriously and miraculously saves and yet effectually displays the condemnation of the sinner. Jesus said he came not to bring peace but a sword (Matthew 10:34) and is still the Prince of Peace (Isaiah 9:6) who gave His disciples supernatural peace (John 14:27). Yielding to Christ enables us to carry on His ministry in spite of the persecution. Like David, like Paul and Silas, our message continues despite the persecution. *Blessed are those who are persecuted because of righteousness for theirs is the kingdom of Heaven* (Matthew 5:10).

If God could turn some of us inside out, he might send us to turn the world upside down. (Leonard Ravenhill)

The message and ministry of the Gospel is opposite of the culture. It is light in darkness. It is hope in despair. It is life in death. It is healing in sickness. It is liberty to the religious. The message and ministry of the Gospel is the fragrance of God to those being saved, but a stench of damnation and misery to those continuing in death. We should not be surprised when culture rejects the Gospel; it is not popular nor comfortable. It is telling the person ridden with the cancer of sin to continue in sickness no more. It is telling the darkness to not exist any longer. It is proclaiming the end of powerless rituals to the religious. This Gospel turns the world upside down. It does not need to be watered down, and it is just as relevant as it ever has been or will be. Preach and minister the Gospel and join the company of those who have gone before us.

Day Sixty-One

HELP!

Likewise, the Spirit also helps in our weaknesses. For we do not know what we should pray for as we ought, but the Spirit Himself makes intercession for us with groanings which cannot be uttered.
Romans 8:26, NKJV

The Holy Spirit, our advocate with the Father, stands ready to help you today. Praying in the Spirit is praying the will of God over the circumstances in your life. Many times our prayers are for our own motives, and *We do not know what we should pray* (James 4:3). But praying in the Holy Spirit is yielding to Divine help and Divine prayer.

Paul uses a compound word for "help" in this passage of Scripture. The Greek describes help much like a lifeguard that rushes to a drowning victim, wrestling and striving with him or her until the person is safe. God comes and strives and wrestles with us until we yield fully to His grace and power in our lives. He pulls us into His secret place of safety.

Instead of praying and wrestling with God over your plans to improve your life, try yielding to the heavenly language and a heavenly time of prayer. It is in this place of surrender we find our help. This heavenly prayer is our refreshing and our rest from the struggles of this world (Isaiah 28:11-12). In this life of prayer, yielding to God transports us from turmoil into the secret place in His shadow of cool, refreshing winds (Psalm 91:1-2). He becomes our fortress of safety and protection.

I was enabled in secret prayer to raise my soul to God, with desire and delight. It was indeed a blessed time. All my past sorrows seemed kindly to disappear, and I "remembered no more the sorrow, for joy." O, how sweetly, and with what an affectionate tenderness the soul confides in the Rock of Ages, knowing He will "never leave it nor forsake it," and that He will cause "all things to work together for good! (David Brainerd)

The Holy Spirit helps us in that we do not what to pray. The Spirit knows and understands what the will of God is (Romans 8:27). Thus, the Holy Spirit teaches us what to pray. He helps us in our weakness. We are not only weak in that we do not know the will of God, but our lack of understanding of His will leaves us weak to do His will. We lack the power to accomplish His will because we have not had a revelation of His will. And so, the Holy Spirit, by prayer in the Spirit, illuminates our mind and our spirit to the will of God, and He enables us to accomplish that desire of God revealed (Philippians 2:13). The Holy Spirit helps us in that He overcomes our weakness of striving. When we do not know the will of God we become anxious and worrisome over the plans of tomorrow. The Spirit of God reveals this will of God, intercedes through us according to this will of God, empowers us to accomplish the will of God, and also removes the obstacle of unbelief. We are weak at entering the promise of God because of unbelief. The Holy Spirit measures to us the faith needed to accomplish the purposes of God that are revealed as we pray in the Spirit. Thus, Jude says: *But you, beloved, building yourselves up on your most holy faith, praying in the Holy Spirit* (Jude 1:20, NKJV).

The Holy Spirit is ready to help you in your time of need. Rest in God by praying in the Spirit!

Day Sixty-Two

Mind-Blowing Work

Now to Him who is able to do exceedingly abundantly above all that we ask or think, according to the power that works in us, to Him be glory in the church by Christ Jesus to all generations, forever and ever. Amen.
Ephesians 3:20-21, NKJV

God wants to blow your mind! I often find that as Christians, if we cannot figure something out in our natural mind, we discount it and consider it "mystical." Could it be that our skepticism about God limits our faith in God? Is it possible that because we don't understand something in our mind we may disregard the very working of God in our midst?

Paul describes a work of God in our lives that is beyond anything we could even think of on our own. Do we need to place a prerequisite on God of our full understanding of His fullness before we yield to His plan? We cannot begin to comprehend the greatness of salvation, a virgin birth, ascension, resurrection, Christ's return, and yet, when it comes to the "power that works in us," we limit the expanse of all that God wants to do because of our inability to figure it out with our natural mind.

Notice Paul says this mind-blowing work of God in us is in direct proportion to the power that is working within us. If your skepticism has limited your faith and the power of God at work in you, it will limit the work of God through you. God is not shocked by our skepticism. He simply says we can continue to live in limited power (if you choose). However, if you want the fullness of His power at work in your life and through your life, there is a mind-blowing work of God in and through your life available as you yield.

It is abundantly clear that the performance of mighty works – signs, wonders, and miracles – belongs with the gospel proclamation. The early Christians testified and performed signs and wonders. The proclamation, therefore, is powerful word and miraculous deed (both by the Holy Spirit), which bear witness to the gospel. (J. Rodman Williams)

Eliminate the barriers of unbelief. Eliminate the obstacles of self and pride. God is able to do a mind-blowing work in and through your life! We are far too easily pleased with temporal satisfactions and only the power to get out of bed in the morning. God has made available His blessings and the very power that formed what our visible eye beholds out of nothing. We have become so mesmerized and lost in a daze by the speed of life that we miss the significance of what God is willing to do, wanting to do, and able to do in and through our yielded lives. Look beyond the ability and strength He has given you to get out of bed or hold down a job. We settle for ordinary when God is working super-celestial. Are we operating at level to push a child's toy car across the room when God is wanting us to fly a spacecraft into the galaxies beyond?

Have you seen God in His majesty? His splendor is indescribable. His glory is undeniable. His holiness is matchless. His righteousness radiates beyond all illumination. His love is beyond remarkable. His joy inexpressible. His power is limitless. Our God is able!

Day Sixty-Three

Pursuit of God

Not that I have already attained, or am already perfected; but I press on, that I may lay hold of that for which Christ Jesus has also laid hold of me. Brethren, I do not count myself to have apprehended; but one thing I do, forgetting those things which are behind and reaching forward to those things which are ahead, I press toward the goal for the prize of the upward call of God in Christ Jesus. Philippians 3:12-14, NKJV

One of the hardest things for many believers is to forget the past. Whether we are ensnared in the faults of others or our own shortcomings, we find ourselves in bondage. Paul said that we should not give the enemy a foothold (Ephesians 4:27). The Greek in this verse indicates a foothold is a stronghold, an inhabited place, a place of power.

Allowing the failures and rejections of the past not only torments you and keeps you in bondage, but it creates a fortified dwelling in your mind for the enemy to wreak havoc on your life. Simply put, a stronghold is the result of the past taking territory today and devastating your future.

God has an incredible calling on your life. Pressing toward the goal requires first that we forgive and forget what lies behind. Sometimes those things that become strongholds are even good things—successes that ensnare us in pride. Let them all go. Paul considered even His successes as loss compared to Christ (Philippians 3:8).

Our focus must be single: *but one thing I do.* We cannot become distracted by too many affections but must have singleness of heart and mind. Forget what lies behind and press toward the goal. Our heavenly goal is obtaining Christ. Our call is a heavenly call to enjoy Him for eternity. Today is the day of reconciliation. Let go of the past and step into your future. Do not allow your past to rob you of your future any longer. You are no longer defined by your past, and who you are today is not who you are becoming tomorrow. God is transforming your life.

He had said that he aimed and eagerly aspired at the resurrection of the dead through fellowship in the Cross of Christ. He adds, that he has not as yet arrived at this. At what? At the attainment of having entire fellowship in Christ's sufferings, having a full taste of the power of his resurrection, and knowing him perfectly. He teaches, therefore, by his own example, that we ought to make progress, and that the knowledge of Christ is an attainment of such difficulty, that even those who apply themselves exclusively to it, do nevertheless not attain perfection in it so long as they live. (John Calvin)

Calvin is expounding here that we never arrive at perfection in this life. We must continually press on, pushing through the distractions and obtaining Christ on that Great Day. There is no spiritual retirement to sit and sour over past regrets. There is no opportunity to grow lazy in your present. It requires continual spiritual determination to lay aside the attachments of this life to fully obtain Christ.

We have no more time to allow yesterday to define us. The clock is quickly fleeing away, and thus, every effort must be made to know Him, enjoy Him, and glorify Him.

Day Sixty-Four

Overflowing Joy

Whom having not seen you love. Though now you do not see Him, yet believing, you rejoice with joy inexpressible and full of glory.
1 Peter 1:8, NKJV

Are you full of joy in your relationship with Christ? Have you found that the joy of your salvation has lost its glory?

David found himself in misery from sinful choices. His prayer of repentance included the appeal that God *restore unto me the joy of your salvation* (Psalm 51:12).

We receive God's Word with joy (Matthew 13:20). Heaven has great joy when sinners are born again (Luke 15:7). Jesus desires for us to live with overflowing joy (John 15:11). We see throughout the Bible that our salvation should be an abundantly joyful salvation. However, throughout life and circumstances, our joy decreases, and like David we must come to Christ for a restoration of joy.

Peter describes the level of joy we ought to have. It is inexpressible and full of glory. It is unspeakable and unimaginable. It is joy that is described in Psalm 126, a joy that fills my mouth with laughter. There is no other way to speak of this joy but to laugh. And this overflowing laughter is full of praise, honor, and magnifying God. Have you been filled with such inexpressible joy? "God is most glorified when I am most satisfied with Him" (John Piper).

It may be said of Christians that they do in fact rejoice; they are happy. The people of the world often suppose that religion makes its professors sad and melancholy. That there are those who have not great comfort in their religion, no one indeed can doubt; but this arises from several causes entirely independent of their religion. Some have melancholy temperaments, and are not happy in anything. Some have little evidence that they are Christians, and their sadness arises not from religion, but from the want of it. But that true religion does make its possessors happy... (Albert Barnes)

Truly discovering Christ is to find the greatest of all joys. It does not mean that sadness in life does not come, but in the sadness, we discover new depths of Christ's joy. For the joy that was set before Him, He endured the cross (Hebrews 12:2). Even at the apex of torture and neglect that any could experience, Christ obtained the joy set before Him. This joy was greater than any of the works He completed that day on the cross or through His resurrection. This joy was greater than His fellowship with the disciples before or during His ascension. His joy was the very presence of His Father. It was the anointing of the Holy Spirit that would cover Him, raise Him up, and seat Him in heavenly places. *Therefore God, Your God, has anointed You with the oil of gladness more than Your companions* (Hebrews 1:9, NKJV).

Christ is now pouring out this same anointing oil upon us. This same Spirit of joy is available. It came first on the Day of Pentecost (Acts 2:33) and is still being lavishly poured out on hungry hearts today!

Day Sixty-Five

Heavenly Construction

But you, beloved, building yourselves up on your most holy faith, praying in the Holy Spirit, keep yourselves in the love of God, looking for the mercy of our Lord Jesus Christ unto eternal life.
Jude 1:20-21, NKJV

Have you ever watched a large building as it is constructed? There is incredible detail and planning that goes into every construction. The same is true of our spiritual building. We are each being built into a dwelling place for God (Ephesians 2:22). Jude gives us insight to ensure our building is structurally sound.

In Matthew 7, Jesus describes the man who built his house upon the sand. When the storms of life came, his destruction was imminent. Jesus likened the man to everyone who hears His words but does not practice them.

Jude's instruction is that we must continually pray in the Spirit, keeping ourselves in the love of God. As we pray in the Spirit, we are praying the Word and will of God over our lives. As we do this, we are "building an edifice" as the Greek in this verse describes. We are constructing and establishing our lives firmly in the love of God.

Praying in the Spirit takes us deeper into the love of God, for it is the Holy Spirit that reveals God's love to us (Romans 5:5). Praying in the Spirit is allowing God to do the construction work of our lives (Psalms 127:1) so that our efforts are not spent in vain.

The Bible says we are to flow together with one mind, one heart, one accord and one purpose. As we pray in the Spirit, the love of God is poured out and released in our lives. This incredible, supernatural love is the source of unity in the Body of Christ. Keep yourself in the love of God, praying in the Holy Spirit. (Frank Bailey)

Are there areas of your life with "under construction" signs but no work being accomplished? There is a children's song with the lyrics: "He's still working on me. To make me what I ought to be. It took him just a week to make the moon and the stars; the sun and the earth and Jupiter and Mars; How loving and patient He must be; 'Cause He's still working on me."

Praying in the Spirit is cooperating with and yielding to the Master Builder of your life. He has the perfect design laid out before the foundations of the world, and He will establish you perfectly and completely. He even empowers us to be a part of the process to yield and be edified in the Spirit.

The corporate body is also edified as you pray in the Spirit together. Just as you are edifying yourself, you are flowing in unity with one another. Praying in the Spirit removes the barriers of miscommunication and personal agendas. It removes that temptation to pray prayers motivated by self-gain. It is a beautiful dependence upon God to build His house, brick by brick, person by person, being united in the Spirit.

Day Sixty-Six

Acts of Power

God also bearing witness both with signs and wonders, with various miracles, and gifts of the Holy Spirit, according to His own will?
Hebrews 2:4, NKJV

The following is an excerpt from Maria Woodworth-Etter's book *Signs and Wonders* describing some of her meetings.

Besides the mighty miracles of healing, God has shown many other signs of His mighty presence and the soon coming of the Lord. In many ways the Holy Spirit has signified that we were near the end. Sometimes during the preaching, God's power would settle down on the saints until some were melted to tears; others saw wonderful visions of His coming glory. Sometimes Sister Etter was held like a statue, unable to utter a word. Other times she stood weeping over the people, while the power of God swept over all like the tide of a great ocean. Around the altar souls saw visions of Him who is walking today among the candlesticks, holding "the seven stars in His right hand" (Rev 2:1). Numbers seems to hear that "voice as the sound of many waters" (Rev 1:15) and like John fell at His feet as dead. The unsaved, beholding the shining faces of those lying as dead men in the presence of God, wept and said, "These are strange things." Sometimes the Spirit would move like a gentle breeze, fanning every soul with the breath of heaven, then send torrents of weeping over the lost until it seemed to some that the very shades of the dark "tribulation" cloud was casting a shadow all around us.

It is the will of God that you be used in a mighty way by the Holy Spirit to share the Gospel message confirmed by signs and wonders. I do not believe that Jesus is coming back for a church operating in less power than the church He left. Greater things are available to us in these days (John 14:12), and those who choose to yield to the Holy Spirit are experiencing a harvest of souls and confirming acts of power.

To believe against hope is the root of the gift of miracles; and I owe this testimony to our beloved church, that apostolic powers are there manifested. We have had undeniable proofs thereof in the unequivocal discovery of things, persons, and circumstances, which could not humanly have been discovered, in the healing of maladies in themselves incurable, such as cancers, consumptions, when the patient was in the agonies of death, all by means of prayer, or of a single word. (Count Nicolaus Ludwig Zinzendorf)

God Himself bears witness concerning the testimony of Jesus with signs and wonders. He uses imperfect vessels to proclaim the message concerning perfect Savior, and then He comes with signs and wonders to testify. He is a wonderful God, and the message is a wonderful Gospel that is demonstrated in wonderful miracles.

Even more, God demonstrates His testimony with spiritual gifts that are diverse yet distributed by the Spirit for the profit of all (1 Corinthians 12). God uses these gifts to testify of Christ for the profit of all. There are a diversity of gifts to address the diversity of people and display the diversity of Christ. Yet in all, Christ is glorified and the Gospel is advanced!

Day Sixty-Seven

Quality Time

Rejoice always, pray without ceasing, in everything give thanks; for this is the will of God in Christ Jesus for you. Do not quench the Spirit.
1 Thessalonians 5:16-19, NKJV

Can you say with David, *my soul longs for, even faints for the courts of my God.* (Psalm 84:2). David cherished his time with the Lord; time that was spent for much of His life watching sheep or running for his life. Even in his sin, David cried, *Do not cast me away from your presence, and do not take your Holy Spirit from me.* (Psalm 51:11).

We have the opportunity to come boldly into the presence of the Lord (Hebrews 4:16) because of the propitiation Christ has made for us. As our propitiation, Christ became our sacrifice. Let us not waiver from our very purpose, but, with great diligence, pursue the presence of God. May we spend such quality time with Him that we know His heart, His thoughts, and His cares. Oh, that we would have the heart of God that is developed by time with Him.

Jonathan Edwards said this in his "Resolution #22:"

Resolved, to endeavor to obtain for myself as much happiness, in the other world, as I possibly can, with all the power; might, vigor, and vehemence, yea violence, I am capable of, or can bring myself to exert, in any way that can be thought of.

To enjoy God, to pray and seek after Him, to not quench or grieve the Holy Spirit, and to do all with great endeavor is to glorify God forever. Ask God today to increase your spiritual appetite. Let him increase your capacity for prayer and worship. Today, may He stir a longing for His presence within you — more than you have known before.

If your heart takes more pleasure in reading novels, or watching TV, or going to the movies, or talking to friends, rather than just sitting alone with God and embracing Him, sharing His cares and His burdens, weeping and rejoicing with Him, then how are you going to handle forever and ever in His presence? You'd be bored to tears in heaven, if you're not ecstatic about God now! (Keith Green)

Rejoicing continually leaves no room for complaining. Praying continually leaves no room for a powerless life. Thankful in all things leaves no room for offense. The Spirit's fire is extinguished when we complain, walk in spiritual apathy and timidity, and are ensnared by offense. Rejoicing, praying, and thanksgiving are fuel for the fire. Rejoicing here is an exceeding, passionate praise. We are to pray according to God's Word continually. Thanksgiving is made in all circumstances in the light of Christ's sacrifice and resurrection. The work of the Spirit through these will fan the flame and enliven passion.

Enter boldly today into His presence with rejoicing, praying, and thanksgiving. He will reveal Himself to you in greater ways and you will enjoy Him more as He does.

Day Sixty-Eight

Walking in the Spirit

I say then: Walk in the Spirit, and you shall not fulfill the lust of the flesh.
Galatians 5:16, NKJV

How true it is that everyone follows somebody. We can choose to follow
our carnal, old nature, or we can follow the direction of the Holy Spirit.
Jesus taught us that the Spirit of Truth would guide us into all truth
(John 16:13). Jesus told us that we would know the truth, and the truth
would set us free (John 8:32). Thus, it is of great importance that we
follow diligently after the Holy Spirit who longs for us to walk in truth
and in freedom.

It is when we follow our carnal nature we are bound to the lusts of the
flesh. Paul taught us in Romans 6 that we are dead to our sinful nature
and should not take up the bondage of this carnality again. To the
Galatians he asked, who had bewitched them. Did the life in Christ that
was begun by the Spirit now become a work of the flesh? (Galatians 3)

In order to walk in the Spirit, we must first have relationship and
fellowship with the Holy Spirit (2 Corinthians 13:14). This fellowship is a
supernatural partnership, much like a marriage. Our journey begins with
a specified destination. Our goal is to take hold of Christ (Philippians
3:14). Our journey must be one of balance. When our balance is off, we
fall. Balance in the Spirit comes from walking a life of faith. Just like our
natural senses keep us balanced, so also does our spiritual perception.
Faith, or balance, comes as we hear the word of God, the message
concerning Christ (Romans 10:17).

Walking in the Spirit requires observation. Assaults, obstacles, and
distractions will come our way, but we maintain our focus. We must lay
aside every weight and run with our eyes fixed on Christ (Hebrews 12).
Observation allows us to be understanding when a snare of offense has
been set. We are able to avoid the trap of the enemy as we remain
vigilant in our observation. We see the situation for what it really is—an
attack from the enemy to stop our journey from advancing.

Walking in the Spirit takes action. If you are going to walk somewhere,
you have to get going. Our motivation comes from the Spirit's work in
our hearts. Our energy to get there is derived from His power in our

lives. The navigation and route are ordered by Him, and He sets our feet in motion. Our muscles, bones, joints, nerves, circulatory system, and all the functions of our spiritual life are set in motion by the Spirit's work. We must walk. Follow the Spirit's direction, and He will lead you safely.

I remember an incident a gentleman told me he once saw upon a bridge over a river. A man was driving a flock of fat lambs, when something met them and hindered their passage. In reaction, one of the lambs leaped upon the wall of the bridge and, his legs slipping from under him, fell into the stream. Seeing him, the rest, one after another, leaped over the bridge into the stream and were all, or almost all, drowned. Those that were behind did not know what was to become of them that were gone before, but thought that they might venture to follow their companions regardless. As soon as they were over the wall and falling headlong, the case was altered. And so it is with unconverted carnal men. (Richard Baxter)

Day Sixty-Nine

Seasons of Refreshing

Repent therefore and be converted, that your sins may be blotted out, so that times of refreshing may come from the presence of the Lord,
Acts 3:19, NKJV

Throughout time, there have been seasons of unique refreshing from the Lord. We can experience the refreshing of the Lord at any time in our journey with Him; however, there are times in history in which God has worked a greater restitution or refreshing for His people.

Acts 3:19 gives instruction on the importance of a repentant life. As Jesus spoke to the Ephesian church, *Nevertheless I have this against you, that you have left your first love* (Revelation 2:4), we also, at times, forsake our first love. The instruction the Church of Ephesus received was to *repent and do the first works* (Revelation 2:5). What were these first works?

Jumping back both in history and Scripture, we find the launch of the Church of Ephesus in Acts 19. Paul spent two years teaching eight hours a day to those who were "charter members." There was great saturation in the presence of God and in His Word during these first years of the church. So great was the ministry of this church, that God worked "extraordinary miracles" (Acts 19:11) through Paul. The Church of Ephesus became a revival center that birthed many other churches. On all accounts, it was a healthy church, but over time, it declined in health. Sure, it still had recognition and notoriety. Jesus even addressed them specifically in Revelation, praising them for their patience and discerning false teachers. Yet, they had lost the most important thing — their first love. May we rekindle our first love. Repent, and ask God to restore those first works of love and passion for Him.

I received a mighty baptism of the Holy Ghost...the Holy Spirit descended upon me in a manner that seemed to go through me, body and soul. I could feel the impression, like a wave of electricity, going through and through me. Indeed it seemed to come in waves and waves of liquid love, for I could not express it in any other way. It seemed like the very breath of God...No words can express the wonderful love that was shed abroad in my heart. I wept aloud with joy and love...I literally bellowed out the unutterable gushings of my heart. These waves came over me, and over me, and over me, one after the other, until I recollect I cried out, "I shall die if these waves continue to pass over me." I said, "Lord, I cannot bear any more;" yet I had no fear of death. (Charles Finney)

Times of revival come from His presence. The word used by Luke for "presence" is the word meaning "face." It's a direct connection to the shewbread in the tabernacle. Jesus called himself the bread from heaven (John 6:51). He is the living bread, or the living presence, that we feast on and find refreshing. His body, symbolized by the unleavened bread at the Passover meal, was broken for you and I, and it gave us access into the Most Holy Place — life behind the veil. This is a life of refreshing and revival.

His reviving presence restores us to a place of wholeness and newness. He removes the effects of sin and refreshes us in His presence.

Day Seventy

All About Him

And my speech and my preaching were not with persuasive words of human wisdom, but in demonstration of the Spirit and of power, that your faith should not be in the wisdom of men but in the power of God.
1 Corinthians 2:4-5, NKJV

Paul's message was an uncompromising Gospel of Truth, for it is the power of God for salvation (Romans 1:16). And this Gospel message was confirmed by external, visible miraculous workings of the Spirit's power. How imperative it is that man's faith not rest in our well-crafted words, but in the ability of the Spirit to work what the Gospel says He will do.

Jim Shaddix in *The Passion Drive Sermon* shares the following truth:

Having settled the issue of preaching content in his (Paul's) heart and mind, he refused to present his message in a way that was dependent upon the empowerment of wise and persuasive arguments, personal popularity and ability, or any other form of self-reliance. Although he came in a very unostentatious way, he was able to display genuine spiritual power because of the work of God's Spirit in and through him. Such should be the confession of preachers in every age so that only God gets the glory in their preaching. After all, it is all about Him.

Each of us are preachers of the Gospel message. We communicate through our actions or inactions. We communicate in what we say or do not say. We communicate every day to those around us who are watching and waiting diligently for the reason of our hope (1 Peter 3:15). Determine that you will preach your message with the power of the Spirit, and forsake a self-reliant message. God will give you the words and the working of His power (Jeremiah 1:7-8).

We must give up the grand distinctions of the schoolmen and all the lettered technicalities of men who have studied theology as a system, but have not felt the power of it in their hearts. When the good old truth is once more preached by men whose lips are touched as with a live coal from off the altar, this shall be the instrument, in the hand of the Spirit, for bringing about a great and thorough revival of religion in the land. (Charles Spurgeon)

When Peter and John were arrested for healing the lame man, the religious leaders marveled at their words and perceived that they were uneducated and untrained, but they realized they had been with Jesus (Acts 4:13). Have you been with Jesus? As Spurgeon says in the above quote, has He taken a coal from the altar that is aflame with God's holy fire, and touched your lips? Let His Word resound from your lips. Let it be said of you, you have been with Jesus.

The religious leaders knew Peter and John had been with Jesus because their lives had been affected and looked like Jesus, how they responded to persecution looked like Jesus, their ministry to the lame man looked like Jesus' ministry, and they healed in the name of Jesus. They preached of Jesus, and their testimony before the religious leaders was of Jesus. The power of the Gospel of Christ was pouring out of every pore, and it affected everyone around.

Day Seventy-One

The Workman of God

I have been crucified with Christ; it is no longer I who live, but Christ lives in me; and the life which I now live in the flesh I live by faith in the Son of God, who loved me and gave Himself for me.
Galatians 2:20, NKJV

Revival begins at the cross. It is the crucifixion of *I*. *I* have been crucified with Christ. This death to self is personal, it is intentional, and it is permanent. Crucifixion is no joking matter. It fully and permanently puts an end to the life of the one hanging on the cross. It is a brutal end to self. Christ became our sacrifice, and in His steps, we must also die daily (1 Corinthians 15:31) to our selfish desires and conduct.

Psalm 116:15, says: *Precious in the eyes of the Lord is the death of His saints.* As we lay our lives upon the altar of sacrifice, offering ourselves as a living sacrifice (Romans 12:1-2), it is pleasing and precious to God.

Watchman Nee in *The Character of God's Workman* shares the following:

To one who does the work of the Lord, his personal life matters much with respect to his work. What he in his character, habit and conduct is essential to his being used of God. This is something to which we need to pay close attention. It speaks of the formation of our nature and the cultivation of our habit. It is more than merely having an experience before God, it involves the forming of character. The Lord has to create a new character in us. In many areas of life we need to be exercised before the Lord until there be developed in us new habits. These things have more to do with our outward man for it is there that we are re-created so as to be fit for the Master's use.

The Lord desires to put to death (Colossians 3:5) those things that are carnal in our character and our habits and cause us to be completely sanctified — spirit, soul, and body-- until His coming (1 Thessalonians 5:23). We are to take up our cross and follow Him (Matthew 16:24) and be prepared to use the cross as needed.

Once more, never think that you can live to God by your own power or strength; but always look to and rely on him for assistance, yea, for all strength and grace. (David Brainerd)

The permanent nature of crucifixion does away with the old self. I no longer live, but Christ lives in me. When Christ takes us residence in a crucified believer, as it were, He brings with Him the resurrection life that quickened Him out of the tomb. Christ does not come to abide in a lifeless person, unemotional, disengaged, spiritually apathetic; He comes to bring resurrection life to the one fully yielded and surrendered to Him. He awakens the whole of a man to heavenly realities. Christ immerses believers into His anointing that breaks off every yoke and liberates from every grave cloth. The fragrance of His name imputed upon the believer brings the fragrances of the oil of heaven. When Christ comes to crucified believer, the believer is fully yielded, surrendered to purposes of Christ, and can be used by Him in this life of faith.

Day Seventy-Two

Unction to Function

For it is God who works in you both to will and to do for His good pleasure.
Philippians 2:13, NKJV

Paul addresses the Philippians with this crucial understanding: It is God who gives the power of desire and the power to accomplish His will. The reason God does this? It is for His good pleasure.

God takes delight in transforming sinners. In fact, it is the greatest display of His glory to redeem fallen man. He takes a man or woman that has a heart of evil (Jeremiah 17:9), draws them in (John 6:44), convicts them (John 16:8), and begins this transforming work from justification through sanctification to glorification. It is impossible in our own strength and ability to have a desire to fulfill God's Word and even more impossible to live according to the Word if we had a desire. It requires God to fully do a supernatural work within us.

He justifies us: declares us righteous. Even though we are guilty, because of Christ's sacrifice we become the righteousness of God in Christ (Romans 8:33; 2 Corinthians 5:21).

Our justification is then lived out through sanctification. Those who are truly born again begin to bear the fruit of repentance (Matthew 3:8). Sanctification is the journey of our carnal nature being transformed from glory to glory (2 Corinthians 3:18) in the image of Christ (Romans 8:29). This process requires us daily to submit to the will of God. This requires the supernatural power of God at work in our lives. He changes our desires and gives us the ability to live His desires (Psalm 37:4).

And some day we will be glorified at Christ's return (Romans 8:30) or the moment we cross from this life to the next. We will no longer carry the limited nature of our flesh but take on immortality (1 Corinthians 15:54) and the radiance of Christ. Even so, come quickly, Lord Jesus! (Revelation 22:20).

God is at work in the life of the believer. He is working for His pleasure according to His counsel regarding your life. He has your best interest in mind, for it His own will that He is working. He is transforming your heart to His will. He is changing your desires to His will. The old nature is dead, and, little by little, you begin reflecting His nature. He continues His work from your will to your motivation and values. He transforms your desires and those things that motivate you to act. He gives both the "will", or desire, along with the "do", or motivation and ability.

God wants more than His children to be stirred by a good sermon; He wants His word to affect our desires, our motives, and our abilities. The addiction you thought would never be broken is now no longer holding you back because He is working both the will and the do. The striving and anxiety has no power in your life any longer because your will and abilities are changed.

Give what you command, and command what you will. (St. Augustine)

Day Seventy-Three

The River is a Person

And he showed me a pure river of water of life, clear as crystal, proceeding from the throne of God and of the Lamb.
Revelation 22:1, NKJV

In Revelation 22:1, we see this wonderful picture of the Holy Spirit. This crystal clear river that flowed from the throne was a prophetic picture of the person of the Holy Spirit.

Think about the power and majesty of a river. Cities are built along rivers to utilize their strength for transportation. Rivers can become a source for electrical power. They can be refreshing and beautiful to enjoy on a hot summer day. The great force of a river contained with its banks is incredible, but to watch in seasons of flood, rivers can be violent and change everything in seconds.

The river of the Holy Spirit is likewise a place of refreshing and beauty. We can enjoy the waters of refreshing, of cleansing, and renewal from the Spirit of God. The Holy Spirit transports us into the throne room of God. He reveals the majesty of God to us. All of the blessings from above flow to us through the river of the Holy Spirit. He also empowers us for supernatural living. In a moment of time, the great force of the river of God can change everything in our lives. Those areas in which we strive for years, momentarily can be liberated by this river. Ezekiel 47 describes this wonderful river that flows through the church and out into a lost world. Wade out into the waters of His glory today. Launch out a little deeper and find there's a great catch of fish!

The upper room was not a hotel where you checked in and never checked out, which a lot of charismatic-Pentecostal churches have become. They're like hotels in that you just come for the feeling, like a drug. You come, get your high, go sit in the corner and say, "Wow." On the day of Pentecost the fire fell to bring in the harvest. Jesus said, "You'll receive power to be My witnesses." A witness is a demonstrator, somebody who's willing to die for what he believes. So when we walk into town as witnesses, we don't just speak a dead word, but we actually demonstrate by His power that He is alive. The same power that rolled away the stone is right there with us. (Rodney Howard Browne)

The river of God pictured in Ezekiel 47 begins at the altar, and it flows outward. The place of personal transformation begins at the altar. Your personal prayer time, your devotional life, and your worship are the fountainhead for the waters that flow into a lost and hurting world. The river of God is perpetually flowing, but you must step into the waters and become an overflowing river in this world by your personal altar. This is a river to drink of, enjoy, be changed, be empowered, be transported and share with others.

In John 7:37, Jesus spoke of the Holy Spirit in the context of a river of living water that would flow from within. Today He is flowing with great might from the heavenly throne and is flowing into and from the lives of believers who will surrender to His ocean divine.

Day Seventy-Four

Take Heed

Therefore, we must give the more earnest heed to the things we have heard lest we drift away.
Hebrews 2:1, NKJV

There is a story about Yogi Berra, the well-known catcher for the New York Yankees, and Hank Aaron, who at that time was the power hitter for the Milwaukee Braves. The teams were playing in the World Series, and as usual, Yogi was keeping up his ceaseless chatter, intended to pep up his teammates and also distract the Milwaukee batters. As Aaron came to the plate, Yogi tried to distract him by saying, "Henry, you're holding the bat wrong. You're supposed to hold it so you can read the trademark." Aaron didn't say anything, but when the next pitch came, he hit it into the left-field bleachers. After rounding the bases and tagging up at home plate, Aaron looked at Yogi Berra and said, "I didn't come up here to read."

Life is full of distractions. If we are not careful, we can find ourselves easily caught in things we were never intended to focus on. Here the apostle tells us to give more earnest heed, or to pay closer attention to the things we have heard. We can be easily lulled to sleep or distracted by life when we should be giving intentional attention to the Word of God.

The apostle continues by arguing the importance of paying closer attention, *lest we drift away.* The translation of the original text means to "leak out" or "slip away." The implication here is simple: we leak! We are vessels that leak. We leak because of just being sinful in our nature. We leak because we are surrounded by a sinful environment. We leak because we are giving way to others. We leak because of discouragement. We leak because of distractions. The Word of God can easily slip away from us if we do not give it priority in our lives. We must be continually filled.

Saturation is the state of something when no more can be added. As believers, we need perpetual saturation. We must continually saturate in God's Word, saturate in His presence saturate in worship saturate in prayer, and saturate in the fellowship of believers. There is always more of God to discover in the avenues in which He reveals Himself; there is always need of the believer to have more of Him. God has given an eternal, limitless supply of Himself and revelation of Himself to those who will seek after Him.

Ephesians 5:18 tells us to be filled with the Spirit, or as translated from the original, *be being filled with the Spirit*. This is a continual state of receiving and saturating in God. You can never have enough. You are not limited to drink in God's Word in moderation. You cannot have too much of His presence. It is in His Word — in God — that we are transformed. The more you saturate, the more your desires change. The more you saturate, the more your spiritual appetite is stirred.

Nothing less will satisfy Him; nothing less, in the very nature of things, will satisfy us, because nothing less than man's more abundant heed is capable of receiving God's more abundant grace. It is the lack of this taking more earnest heed, the lack of intense earnestness, giving God and religion the first place and the best powers of our life, which is at the root of the feebleness and sickliness of the Christian life. God is speaking to us in His Son, therefore, we ought to take more abundant heed. (Andrew Murray)

Day Seventy-Five

So Great a Salvation

How shall we escape if we neglect so great a salvation…
Hebrews 2:3, NKJV

The greatness of God is revealed in such a wonderfully great salvation. Consider for a moment the greatness of your salvation. Consider its magnificent design that was fashioned before the worlds were formed. God in his Sovereignty and incredible wisdom, saw fit to create man and rescue him from his fallen, sinful state. This salvation was no ordinary salvation through the blood of bulls and goats, but it came at the cost of God's only begotten, the precious Lamb of God.

The greatness of God is revealed in this salvation in that God has sworn according to His good pleasure and counsel to fulfill His covenant. He has consulted no one but Himself and sworn by Himself and sealed us with the precious seal of His own Spirit. Even the Spirit of God confirms to us that we are His children.

The greatness of God is revealed in this salvation in that God Himself, the creator of all things, stepped out of eternity and into humanity to execute redemption's work. He took on the nature of a man, became our sacrifice, and took on the punishment of our sin. God has declared His testimony concerning His son as His voice thundered from Heaven at Christ's baptism and again at the transfiguration, "This is my beloved son…" How great a salvation that its designer, its author, its perfecter, its finisher became its sacrifice and administer of it.

The greatness of God is revealed in this salvation as it redeems from the most awful of sins. This wonderful salvation rescues the worst of the worst, the vilest of the vile, and transforms the horrid into beauty. He makes the ashes into indescribable glory.

The greatness of God is revealed in this salvation in that it does not require great faith and men and women of great position to receive it. This salvation came to all who would call on the name of the Lord. This salvation came with the smallest of faith — faith as simple as to receive the crucified and resurrected Christ. Only the faith of a mustard seed might utterly translate a person from complete despair to incredible eternal bliss.

The greatness of God is revealed in this salvation because it saves from the greatest of all punishments. How great a salvation that rescues the sinner from an eternal torment in eternal hell with eternal weeping, eternal judgment, and eternal bondage to sin. There is, eternal realization of what is truth and what was believed in this life in error, eternal pain and suffering, eternal burning and torture, the eternal smell of death and judgment and sickness, and an ultimate and eternal realization of the greatest of all joys and pleasures was always available but never, and forever not to be, enjoyed.

The tide of compassion was rising higher and higher in His bosom through eternity 'till it overflowed in the fullness of time and God gave His Son. It was for this that the whole world was set up, sun, moon and stars and rolling worlds, hills, mountains, valleys, these are but the boards of the stage on which salvation was to be carried on and when salvation is done, these will be all burned up. (Robert Murray McCheyne)

Day Seventy-Six

Taking Due Care

How shall we escape if we neglect so great a salvation...
Hebrews 2:3, NKJV

Neglect is a powerful word. It is to be uncared for or to allow something to enter disrepair. John Owen describes this as not taking "due care" about it. This word intimates an omission of all the duties that are necessary if we are to retain the Word that has been preached to us.

The apostle in Hebrews 2:1 instructs us to take a more earnest heed, and, here again, he instructs us to not neglect but to take care of what we have received.

Albert Barnes elaborates more on this verse here:

If we neglect - It is not merely if we commit great sins. Not, if we are murderers, adulterers, thieves, infidels, atheists, scoffers. It is, if we merely "neglect" this salvation - if we do not embrace it - if we suffer it to pass unimproved. "Neglect" is enough to ruin a man. A man who is in business need not commit forgery or robbery to ruin himself; he has only to "neglect" his business, and his ruin is certain. A man who is lying on a bed of sickness, need not cut his throat to destroy himself; he has only to "neglect" the means of restoration, and he will be ruined. A man floating in a skiff above Niagara, need not move an oar or make an effort to destroy himself; he has only to "neglect" using the oar at the proper time, and he will certainly be carried over the cataract. Most of the calamities of life are caused by simple "neglect." By neglect of education children grow up in ignorance; by neglect a farm grows up to weeds and briars; by neglect a house goes to decay; by neglect of sowing, a man will have no harvest; by neglect of reaping, the harvest would rot in the fields. No worldly interest can prosper where there is neglect; and why may it not be so in religion? There is nothing in earthly affairs that is valuable that will not be ruined if it is not attended to - and why may it not be so with the concerns of the soul? Let no one infer, therefore, that because he is not a drunkard, or an adulterer, or a murderer, that, therefore, he will be saved. Such an inference would be as irrational as it would be for a man to infer that because he is not a murderer his farm will produce a harvest, or that because he is not an adulterer therefore his merchandise will take care of itself.

We have been graciously and abundantly bestowed the wonderful salvation of God, given free access into His presence, the ability to access

His limitless wisdom and creativity, and yet, we become more enamored with playing in the sandbox while God has given us eternity as our playground.

Consider again today the redemption you have been given. Consider again today the great price that was paid. Consider again today the great access you have been granted. May Christ mesmerize your heart, inflame your mind, stir your emotions, quicken your body, and transform your will yet again as you consider Him and this great salvation. As you take heed of what you have been given in abundance, may your response be abundant praise and adoration of the Author and Finisher of your faith!

Day Seventy-Seven

Who Is Your Running Partner?

You ran well. Who hindered you from obeying the truth? This persuasion does not come from Him who calls you.
Galatians 5:7-8, NKJV

Paul had said to the Corinthian church "bad company corrupts good character." Here again, Paul is reminding believers of the importance of those who influence your life.

When runners are preparing for a race, they do not choose coaches and running partners that tell them they can eat anything they like. Likewise, they do not pick partners that tell them they will not finish or how lazy, selfish, or how horrible they are. Runners know that running a race takes discipline and confidence. Running a race requires practice and preparation. It requires avoiding choices that negatively impact a runner's running ability — like eating a big cake before the run.

The Galatians had been influenced by those preaching in error. In Galatians 3, Paul even presents the question: *O foolish Galatians! Who has bewitched you that you should not obey the truth, before whose eyes Jesus Christ was clearly portrayed among you as crucified?*

Those who influence us should be those running the same race with the same desire and outcome — to obtain Christ. In 1 Corinthians 9, Paul reminds us to run in a way to obtain the prize and not to be disqualified. Hebrews 12 instructs us to lay aside every weight and sin and to focus on Christ in order that we might run the race with endurance. In 2 Timothy 2, we are reminded that obtaining the prize is a result of competing according to the rules. Paul tells us in Philippians 3 that our prize is obtaining Christ.

The law of relationship is crucial. This law is the undeniable reality that those who you are in relationship with will influence your life. Pride says things like: "I can handle it." "They won't affect me." "I'm just ministering to them." "I am stronger than that." The reality is that even the slightest influence can cause you to fall off the track or jump into another lane you were not called to run in.

The righteous should choose his friends carefully, for the way of the wicked leads them astray.

Proverbs 12:26, NKJV

The devil is a cunning persuader. He knows how to enlarge the smallest sin into a mountain until we think we have committed the worst crime ever committed on earth. Such stricken consciences must be comforted and set straight as Paul corrected the Galatians by showing them that their opinion is not of Christ because it runs counter to the Gospel, which describes Christ as a meek and merciful Savior. (Martin Luther)

Like the Galatians, have you found your race affected by those around you? Maybe a sin or weight has your pace or focus off balance. The wonderful Savior has set an example for you. Set your eyes again on the joy of Christ before you, cast off restraint, remove the one who has affected your run, and carry on with the race Christ has set you upon.

Day Seventy-Eight

Clean Hands, Pure Heart

Who may ascend into the hill of the Lord? Or who may stand in His holy place? He who has clean hands and a pure heart, who has not lifted up his soul to an idol, nor sworn deceitfully.
Psalm 24:3-4, NKJV

The Lord is calling His children to ascend the hill of His presence. This is more than a simple religious pilgrimage; He wants fellowship and intimacy. This is not just shadows of His coming. He has come — and calls into His presence.

We are presented in this Psalm with not just ritual cleansings but a sanctification process. Our activity, our meditations, our will, our mind, our emotions, and our language — all must be cleansed. Those who desire to live in the presence of God must be continually changed in these areas. If your hands are unclean, they must be washed in Jesus' blood. If the meditations of your heart are impure, then He must write His words upon your heart. If your soul is consumed by self-worship, then your affections must find delight in Him. If your language is unbecoming, then let Him fill your mouth with blessing. The work of God upon the soul of man will make you fit to ascend His holy hill.

There must be a work of grace in the core of the heart as well as in the palm of the hand, or our religion is a delusion. May God grant that our inward powers may be cleansed by the sanctifying Spirit, so that we may love holiness and abhor all sin. The pure in heart shall see God, all others are but blind bats; stone-blindness in the eyes arises from stone in the heart. Dirt in the heart throws dust in the eyes. (Charles Spurgeon)

To ascend Zion's holy hill, you must first come to the hill of Golgotha where Christ was crucified. To live in God's presence, you must first be cleansed at the cross on Calvary's Hill. It was on that cross that Christ's hands were pierced so that your hands may be clean. It was on the cross that Christ's heart was torn by the centurion's spear so that your heart could be made new. At Calvary, Christ was lifted up so that you might come and worship Him alone. At Calvary, Christ cried out, "Father, forgive them," that you might have His Word of Life flowing from your lips.

Once at Calvary's Hill, you may follow the Lord to the garden tomb where resurrection life will quicken you and send you on your way up the hill of the Lord.

Abstain from every form of evil. Now may the God of peace Himself sanctify you completely; and may your whole spirit, soul, and body be preserved blameless at the coming of our Lord Jesus Christ. He who calls you is faithful, who also will do it (1 Thessalonians 5:22-24, NKJV).

Let every worker learn to say: As the power that worked in Christ, let that power work no less in me. There is no possible way of working God's work aright, but God working it in us (Andrew Murray).

Day Seventy-Nine

An Achan Heart

Get up, sanctify thy people, and say, 'Sanctify yourselves for tomorrow, because thus says the Lord God of Israel: "There is an accursed thing in your midst, O Israel; you cannot stand before your enemies until you take away the accursed thing from among you."'
Joshua 7:13, NKJV

When reading the account of Achan's sin in Joshua, there are a couple of obvious lessons here. The first of the lessons is about not allowing sin in our life. Achan had stolen what God said was cursed. He knew he had done wrong and hid the stolen goods under his tent. The result of this sin was God's wrath manifest in the killing of innocent men at Ai. Achan's sin brought guilt into his own heart, causing him to attempt to hide his sin, but it was known to God. His sin then brought shame and the innocent blood of others onto his family.

It seems so insignificant, though. Achan only had a Babylonian garment, under half a pound of silver, and a wedge of gold weighing about a pound. What was the big deal? It was just a little lie. That is how many respond about sin. It is just a little sin. No one was hurt. There is no justification of sin except for that which comes through the blood of Christ by faith.

Another lesson here is that God does not secretly deal with this sin in a back room of Joshua's tent. The entire camp of Israelites knew someone had sinned, and someone had lied. God could have told Joshua exactly who the culprit was, but instead, it became an opportunity for everyone to learn the value of a sanctified life. The sin in Achan's heart was exposed.

The remedy for the sin reminds of us the great mercy and grace of the Lord today. Joshua called for Achan and his family; the family was stoned and their bodies burned in order than God's anger would be appeased. Thank God for Christ who took our punishment for sin. Though the price has been paid, we do not have an excuse to carry on in sin. The grace of God changes us. The grace of God liberates us.

When Achan and his family were destroyed, the Israelites were victorious. Because the power of sin was destroyed at Calvary, we can now walk in victory! Christ's death and resurrection did more than provide atonement for sin; the power over sin was given to those who are in Christ. We no longer have live in slavery to sin.

Another reality about Achan's heart of sin is the consequence of sin always brings trouble. The Israelites found themselves in the Valley of Achor or the Valley of Trouble because of sin. Sin always costs more, goes farther, and stays longer than you expect. With sin comes brokenness, hurt, offense, bondage, pride, and more. Each of these companions bring trouble, and none of them are worth keeping around. Destroy the sin, and remove the trouble. Acts 3:19-21 describes how Christ will bring times of restoration from the effects of sin when we repent. Repentance sets us on a path of revival, reformation, and restoration.

Times of danger and trouble should be times of reformation. We should look at home, into our own hearts, into our own houses, and make diligent search to find out if there be not some accursed thing there, which God sees and abhors; some secret lust, some unlawful gain, some undue withholding from God or from others. We cannot prosper, until the accursed thing be destroyed out of our hearts, and put out of our habitations and our families, and forsaken in our lives (Matthew Henry).

Day Eighty

It Is Not Hard to Praise Him

While Peter was still speaking these words, the Holy Spirit fell upon all those who heard the word.
Acts 10:44, NKJV

Oh, it was not hard to praise Him. He had become so near and so inexpressibly dear to my heart. Hallelujah! Without effort on my part I began to say: "Glory to Jesus! Glory to Jesus! Glory to Jesus!!!" Each time that I said "Glory to Jesus," it seemed to come from a deeper place in my being than the last, and in a deeper voice, until great waves of "Glory to Jesus" were rolling from my toes up; such adoration and praise I had never known possible. All at once my hands and arms began to shake, gently at first, then violently, until my whole body was shaking under the power of the Holy Spirit. I did not consider this at all strange, as I knew how the batteries we experimented with in laboratory at college hummed and shook and trembled under the power of electricity, and there was the Third Person of the Trinity coming into my body in all His fullness, making me His dwelling, "the temple of the Holy Ghost." Was it any wonder that this poor human frame of mind should quake beneath the mighty movings of His power? How happy I was, Oh how happy! Happy just to feel His wonderful power taking control of my being. Oh Glory! That sacred hour is so sweet to me, the remembrance of its sacredness thrills me as I write. Almost without my notice my body slipped gently to the floor, and I was lying stretched out under the power of God, but felt as though caught up and floating upon the billowy clouds of glory. Do not understand by this that I was unconscious of my surroundings, for I was not, but Jesus was more real and near than the things of earth round about me. The desire to praise and worship and adore Him flamed up within my soul. He was so wonderful, so glorious, and this poor tongue of mine so utterly incapable of finding words with which to praise Him. My lungs began to fill and heave under the power as the Comforter came in. The cords of my throat began to twitch — my chin began to quiver, and then to shake violently, but Oh, so sweetly! My tongue began to move up and down and sideways in my mouth. Unintelligible sounds as of stammering lips and another tongue, spoken of in Isaiah 28:11, began to issue from my lips. This stammering of different syllables, then words, then connected sentences, was continued for some time as the Spirit was teaching me to yield to Him. Then suddenly, out of my innermost being flowed rivers of praise in other tongues as the Spirit gave utterance, and Oh I knew that He was praising Jesus with glorious language, clothing Him with honor and glory which I felt but never could have put into words.

Aimee Semple McPherson, Sister Aimee, as she was known, describes here her baptism in the Holy Spirit. What a blessed and wonderful promise and gift the Father extends to each of us. To the New Testament church, this was the Promise of which Jesus spoke about and commanded them to not leave Jerusalem until they had received it. This was the precious promise that Peter preached about to those gathered at Cornelius's home in Acts 10. This was the wonderful promise that Paul preached about to the Ephesian believers in Acts 19. This promise is for you!

Just as we receive a wonderful salvation, the virgin birth, the crucifixion, the resurrection, miracles, healings, and every facet of our Christianity by faith; even so we receive and understand this promise of the Holy Spirit and divine communication by faith. He has come to give you power. The Comforter has truly come, and He will continue to come and saturate the hungry and thirsty life. Even now as you read the words on this page, He can fill you with overflowing joy and divine life. Go ahead and receive more of Him today!

Day Eighty-One

Outdo with Honor

Be kindly affectionate to one another with brotherly love, in honor giving preference to one another.
Romans 12:10, NKJV

The believer's life should exemplify a life of honor. To protect an outpouring of God's Spirit, a church must operate in honor. Honoring someone or honoring God means to show high esteem or respect.

Paul is instructing us in outdoing one another in honor. In the New King James, it translates "giving preference to one another." The original text paints a picture of looking for ways to intentionally show honor to someone, or outdo one another with honor.

Here are some thoughts about creating a house of honor:

1. Honoring one another is a command. We do not show honor only when we feel someone is deserving. Consider Christ and the honor He gave to us while we were still enemies. He loved us, preferred us, and showed us tender affection when we deserved punishment and judgment.
2. To honor one another Biblically, we must have our Father's perspective. It is easy to see offense or unmet expectations, but Christ compels us to honor in spite of our brother's and sister's shortcomings. Honoring one another releases others from their fears, hurts, and hang ups and brings them into a place of safety and love.
3. The punishment of sin was met at the cross. There is a difference between consequence and punishment. Often, when we feel wronged, we seek punishment and justice. Honor seeks to love and restore. Christ did not remove the consequences of sin, but He did take our punishment for sin. Honoring one another seeks to bring restoration and reconciliation, not retribution.
4. To honor someone is to see them through the lens of faith in Christ. As you honor someone, you may be the only reflection of the heavenly perspective of Christ that they will see. As you reflect this honor to them by faith in Christ, someone may actually see themselves as Christ sees them.
5. A lifestyle of honor requires us to live to a higher standard. We

cannot stay in the brokenness, pity, guilt, remorse, and defeated mindset and way of living. Honor requires embracing a heavenly lifestyle.

We should be forward to take notice of the gifts, and graces, and performances of our brethren, and value them accordingly, be more forward to praise another, and more pleased to hear another praised, than ourselves; ...going before, or leading one another in honour; so some read it: not in taking honour, but in giving honour. "Strive which of you shall be most forward to pay respect to those to whom it is due, and to perform all Christian offices of love (which are all included in the word honour) to your brethren, as there is occasion (Matthew Henry).

Day Eighty-Two

He is Coming Soon!

*Behold, I tell you a mystery: We shall not all sleep, but we shall all be changed —
in a moment, in the twinkling of an eye, at the last trumpet. For the trumpet
will sound, and the dead will be raised incorruptible, and we shall be changed.*
1 Corinthians 15:51-52, NKJV

Christ's coming is quickly approaching. The first century disciples at
Christ's ascension were instructed that Christ would return in like
manner. They lived their lives as though Christ was coming in their
lifetime. We should live likewise.

The parable of the virgins reminds us how easy it is to become
disillusioned and fall asleep. We do not prepare and make ourselves
ready when the groom is coming. That our betrothed seems to be
delayed does not mean He is not returning or that He has somehow
forgotten. The Father knows the day and the time of the wedding feast,
and we must remain ready.

We will wait for a lot in this life but are easily put off with living
righteously as we wait for Christ's coming. We wait for paychecks. We
wait for the doctor. We wait for our tax returns. We wait for shipments.
We wait for our television show. We wait for sporting events. We wait
for the movies. God, help us to wait expectantly for Christ.

*Christ's first coming was without external pomp or display of power, and yet in
truth there were few who could endure its test. Herod and all Jerusalem with
him were stirred at the news of the wondrous birth. Those who supposed
themselves to be waiting for Him showed the fallacy of their professions by
rejecting Him when He came. His life on earth was like a winnowing fan that
sifted the great heap of religious profession, and only a few could survive the
process. But what will His second coming be? What sinner can endure to think
of it? "He shall strike the earth with the rod of his mouth, and with the breath of
his lips he shall kill the wicked" (Isaiah 11:4). In Gethsemane when He said to
the soldiers, "I am he," they fell backward. What will happen to His enemies
when He will reveal Himself more fully as the "I Am"? His death shook earth
and darkened heaven. What will be the dreadful splendor of that day when as the
living Savior He will summon the living and the dead before Him? O that the
terrors of the Lord would persuade men to forsake their sins and kiss the Son in
case He is angry! Though a lamb, He is still the lion of the tribe of Judah, tearing
the prey in pieces; and though He does not break the bruised reed, yet He will*

break His enemies with a rod of iron and dash them to pieces like a potter's vessel. None of His foes shall stand before the tempest of His wrath or hide themselves from the sweeping hail of His indignation. But His beloved blood-washed people look for His appearing with joy; in this living hope they live without fear. To them He sits as a refiner even now, and when He has tested them they shall come forth as gold. Let us examine ourselves and make our calling and election sure, so that the coming of the Lord may not be the case of fearful expectations. O for grace to discard all hypocrisy, and to be found of Him sincere and without rebuke on the day of His appearing (Charles Spurgeon).

Christ is coming. I can hear the stallions of heaven preparing. We will soon ride with Him in victory over our enemies, and Christ shall reign eternally as King of kings and Lord of lords!

Day Eighty-Three

Unprecedented Days

You have heard; See all this. And will you not declare it? I have made you hear new things from this time, even hidden things, and you did not know them. Isaiah 48:6, NKJV

Isaiah 43:18-19 echoes this same concept of God doing a new work: *Do not remember the former things, nor consider the things of old. Behold, I will do a new thing, now it shall spring forth; shall you not know it? I will even make a road in the wilderness and rivers in the desert.*

Unprecedented means something never done before or known before. God is doing an unprecedented work in our day. There is a new sound, a new work, and a new creativity. A new work of God requires you to be made new as well. This new wine, or new work, cannot be put into old wineskins.

To walk into the new, unprecedented work of the Lord, you must first let go of the past. Your past does not define you. God has used the past to bring you to where you are today, but He is still at work in you. Today, you can hear new things. You do not have to continue playing the old tapes of hurts, lies, and brokenness. Past successes and victories, though inspiring, fail in comparison to where the Lord is bringing you. To walk into new territory, you must hear the new GPS directions from the Holy Spirit. This requires tuning in more closely and listening more attentively. The path is not previously known. He will direct your steps, but you must give heed to His voice and not venture off the path He has laid. He has made you hear the voice of His Son. In times past, you heard your pride and own desires, but He has made your ears to hear new, unprecedented sounds. You can now hear sounds of worship, sounds of wisdom, sounds of heaven, sounds of prayer, and sounds of His Word that before were like distant tones-- if they were audible at all.

God is making a road in hopeless circumstances. To those who seem lost in the desert, rivers are breaking forth. This is not a mirage but an oasis. It may seem that you have wandered this way in the past and did not see what you now see; however, like the Israelites wandering around the same path for forty years, they saw clearly the path to Canaan as God purged their unbelief. As He purges your unbelief, your eyes can see things that were once hidden. He has now made them plain before you and has caused you to know them through faith in Christ.

There is a road laid out before you. No longer will you walk on a dusty path without markings, for He has laid a highway of holiness on which you will walk. This highway of holiness, though narrow and straight, will lead to the way everlasting. This is the way of the redeemed, Sinners who have been saved by grace and have been placed upon the path of righteousness in Christ. There can be heard the abundant sounds of grace. There can be seen the wonderful workings of life. There can be tasted the refreshing waters of joy.

Christ is like a river in another respect. A river is continually flowing, there are fresh supplies of water coming from the fountain-head continually, so that a man may live by it, and be supplied with water all his life. So, Christ is an ever-flowing fountain; he is continually supplying his people, and the fountain is not spent. They who live upon Christ, may have fresh supplies from him to all eternity; they may have an increase of blessedness that is new, and new still, and which never will come to an end (Jonathan Edwards).

Day Eighty-Four

Praise Your Name Forever

Every day I will bless You, and I will praise Your name forever and ever.
Psalm 145:2, NKJV

The words "praise" and "bless" in the Old Testament have a lot of powerful meanings that might be missed in just reading the text at face value. Our word "praise" can be translated to Hebrew with seven different meanings. Psalm 145 is a great example of this.

"Halal" means to rave and to celebrate wildly with extreme demonstrative worship. It is loud and involves physical movement. This is certainly not a self-conscious praise, rather it is consumed by passion.

Psalm 119:164 says I will "halal" or "praise" you seven times a day. David's rejoicing was a celebration of God and His Word. Seven times a day He would dance about rejoicing and praising God for His Word and His goodness.

This was a perpetual praise, much like the order of praise established in David's tabernacle. This was a place of continual praise to God. God has made His people instruments of perpetual praise. As His children, we have the ability to dance and rejoice before God with songs, shouts, and demonstrations of our praise continually.

Psalm 150 is a Song of "Halal" or praise. Halal, or praise Him with great uninhibited celebration, in His sanctuary, in the mighty heavens, for His mighty deeds, and in proportion to His abundant majesty. Praise Him with the blast of the trumpet, with the nevel and the kinnor, and with the tambourine and dance. Praise Him wildly with the reed pipe, on the high cymbals and the low cymbals. Let everything that has breath praise the Lord with uninhibited praise!

If you have breath in your lungs, you have a reason to dance, shout, and sing with uninhibited praise. As you breathe out your praise, the life of God in you is being released through rejoicing. God is exalted, and your atmosphere is affected. Celebrating God with crazy, unashamed praise brings your body, your words, and your focus into alignment with God's glory. This is a place of breakthrough and transformation. Halal praise aligns your whole being into an exuberant rejoicing of God. Consider today the wonders of His nature, the working of His hands, and the promises of His Word.

He gave them breath, let them breathe his praise. His name is in the Hebrew composed rather of breathings than of letters, to show that all breath comes from him: therefore, let it be used for him. Join all ye living things in the eternal song. Be ye least or greatest, withhold not your praises. What a day will it be when all things in all places unite to glorify the one only living and true God! This will be the final triumph of the church of God. Praise ye the LORD. Once more, Hallelujah! (Charles Spurgeon)

Day Eighty-Five

Increased by God

May the Lord God of your fathers make you a thousand times more numerous than you are, and bless you as He has promised you!
Deuteronomy 1:11, NKJV

God wants to enlarge and expand you. He is at work broadening your influence and your ministry. Isaiah 54 speaks to this increase: *Enlarge the place of your tent, and let them stretch out the curtains of your dwelling.*

Evil is accelerating all around us. Life seems to always be speeding up. The Day of the Lord is approaching more quickly. Now is not the time to sit idly by and be in distress. We are called to occupy and take dominion. We are called to advance the Kingdom.

God's dream and vision set before you has not been placed like the carrot dangled in front of the donkey, only to be taken away. He is a loving Father with every intention of completing the work He has begun in you. God has not called you to continue in lack but to embrace heavenly resources, direction, wisdom, and power.

In 2 King 6, Elisha was facing the chariots and horses of the enemy. The city was surrounded by the enemy. Fear of destruction and death were coming upon the city. Elisha saw supernatural help that others could not see. God had increased their influence, even though the natural eye could not see the help.

We are not always capable of seeing the provision of God in the natural. It is with the eyes of faith that we can see the promise of God for increase and provision. Just like the servant, may we hear the prayer of Jesus: *Father, open their eyes.*

And Elisha prayed, and said, "Lord, I pray, open his eyes that he may see." Then the Lord opened the eyes of the young man, and he saw. And behold, the mountain was full of horses and chariots of fire all around Elisha. (2 Kings 6:17, NKJV)

This was more than wishful thinking; this was reality by faith. God was working on behalf of Elisha, and He is working on your behalf today. Your Helper has come. The Holy Spirit, of whom Christ said is "Another Helper," has come to advocate for you; reveal the Father to you;

empower you; convict you; counsel you; guide you into all truth; and reveal all that is of God to you.

Too often, our so-called spiritual accomplishments, can lead us to a case of the "big head syndrome". When we acknowledge that it all flows from Him and back to Him again, God receives the honor and glory, we experience the blessing of being used by the Lord. Knowing Him personally puts you in touch with His continual help. He is our Helper in every aspect of our lives. (Frank Bailey)

Day Eighty-Six

Jacob's Ladder

Then Jacob awoke from his sleep and said, "Surely, the Lord is in this place, and I did not know it."
Genesis 28:16, NKJV

What a place to be — in the presence of the Lord and not know it. Jacob needed an awakening. In his slumber he was staring the Almighty in the face, and he did not know it. In His dream, God spoke to Jacob regarding the promise made to Abraham. God was at work accomplishing His plan of the ages, and Jacob did not perceive it. In fact, Jacob made a promise with God that was based on his earthly needs: bread, clothing, family. All the while, God was doing a work that would last even to today.

Oh, how we need the awakening of the Lord to bring us out of our sleep. We need to truly hear God's voice and understand His promises. It is just like humans to have an incredible opportunity to experience the very glory of the Lord, miss it, and then to see how what God did in that moment only applies to our very limited present earthly experience. In reality, God is trying to work something much greater. He is accomplishing His eternal plan of the ages in which He has graciously made us a unique part. God is saying the eternal promise to His people will come to pass through our lives, and all we hear about is our food, clothes, and immediate needs.

Today, can you hear the voice of the Lord? *Therefore He says: "Awake, you who sleep, arise from the dead, and Christ will give you light"* (Ephesians 5:14, NKJV). He will open your eyes to His radiance today. You can behold Him in His beauty and be captivated by His glory.

God chose to inhabit the unlikely place. Jacob was not expecting a divine visitation, but God chose the unexpected moment. How often does God reveal Himself in the place we cannot see hope or have a sense of a miracle? It was frequently in the moments of fear where Jesus revealed His glory and challenged their unbelief. Christ does not scorn you or make you an outcast for your limitations of humanity, but rather, He calls you higher and beyond those limitations through faith. God did not chastise Jacob for his slumber in the moment He chose to speak but revealed Himself through it.

The Church must arise from her sleep, but God has not ostracized her for her slumber. He is graciously wooing and calling out for repentance and transformation. Christ loves His bride and desires to reveal Himself more intimately to those who will arise off their beds and run with Him in the night hours. Darkness has covered the earth, but the Radiant One has come and is stirring His bride to awake and to pursue after Him.

The supreme attention of their minds is to the glorious excellencies of God and Christ; and there is very often a ravishing sense of God's love accompanying a sense of His excellence. They rejoice in a sense of the faithfulness of God's promises, as they respect the future eternal enjoyment of Him. (Jonathan Edwards)

Day Eighty-Seven

Acceleration

Then they willingly received Him into the boat, and immediately the boat was at the land where they were going.
John 6:21, NKJV

Jesus had just fed and ministered to the multitudes. The disciples had picked up the leftovers, and the people were amazed by the multiplication of the fish and bread. Now they wanted to force Jesus to be king.

What they did not understand was they were staring the bread that came down from heaven in the face. They were listening to the living bread who could eternally satisfy them. He was already King, but not the king they wanted. He was their miracle, but not the miracle they wanted.

The disciples got into a boat and started out over the Sea of Galilee. Jesus was still on the land while the disciples were now four miles out on the sea. The shoreline had become almost invisible in the distance, and it became much harder to see as a storm started stirring. Before long, the wind was causing the waves to pound against their boat. The air was filled with mist from the water, and Jesus was nowhere to be found.

Like the disciples, thoughts of fear and dread may come as you consider your boat might sink in the midst of the sea. There is worry and anxiety over whether or not the boat can make it back to shore or to the other side. What happens if the boat takes on water? Will the storm grow worse? How long will this continue? Perhaps you have experienced such fear and concern in life's journey. Know that Christ is on His way. The one who just worked a miracle of multiplication is capable of calming the storm.

Across the water, in the midst of a storm, Christ came walking on the water. When He got into the boat, immediately the boat was on land. Four miles into the sea, and when Christ stepped onto their boat, they were immediately at the land.

Christ has come to accelerate the journey and get you to where you are going. He wants to move you into a new season, bring you from the storm and onto the land. The days of just surviving are over, and it is time to excel. You have not been called to hold the fort but to storm the gates of the enemy. Advance the Gospel! Do not give up before your breakthrough. Christ is walking on the water towards your boat. Watch and see what the Lord will continue to do in your life as He accelerates His plan in your life.

That's what lordship is – Christ reigning as supreme authority over our life. Making Jesus Lord of our life is not something passive. It's not a state of being, it's a state of doing. Those whom Jesus recognizes as His own are those who do the will of His Father in heaven (Keith Green).

Day Eighty-Eight

It is Finished

When Jesus had received the sour wine, he said, "It is finished," and he bowed his head and gave up his spirit.
John 19:30, NKJV

In the natural, these are not the words of victory. A conquering king, an all-powerful savior does not proclaim, "It is finished," from the cross. Surely, He could come down. After all, He is the Son of God.

It was the darkest of all hours. The Father had looked away from His Son as Christ took upon Himself the punishment and sins of mankind. Look upon the crucified Christ. He is not shouting profanities, demanding justice, or seeking vengeance. He prays for forgiveness. He speaks to the repentant thief a promise of hope and redemption.

This was not the end of a worn-out life. Christ was freely laying down His life. His head did not drop in anguish, but He gracefully bowed His head. He showed full control and understanding throughout the ordeal. It was now time to give up His spirit. No one took His spirit from Him, but he bowed His head and gave it up.

In His words, "It is finished," are the totality of redemption. He completed the work for which He came. He bore the sins of the world. He became the sacrifice. He took the punishment of God. Because Christ finished His work at the cross, you can have peace with God. Because of Christ's finished work, you can have forgiveness of sin.

The skeletons that haunt you are finished. The guilt of the sins of your past is over. The condemnation you have carried is removed. His finished work redeems, justifies, and cleanses your conscience clean. Christ's finished work brings restoration. The effects of sin's vileness can be removed and new life restored. The power of the cross cleanses and delivers. His blood can remove every stain, and liberate the worst of sinners. There is no bondage greater than the blood of Jesus.There is no history of sin so great that Christ cannot deliver.

Therefore, He is also able to save to the uttermost those who come to God through Him, since He always lives to make intercession for them (Hebrews 7:25, NKJV).

Healing flows from His wounds. He has not only completed His work, but He has brought the reign of sin to a permanent and final end. The power of death is broken. Thanks be to God who gives us victory! By the power of Christ's death and resurrection we are transformed from glory to glory. We are made new and renewed by His grace that has been abundantly poured out.

Seek to be made holier every day; pray, strive, wrestle for the spirit, to make you like God. Be as much you can with God. I declare to you that I had rather be one hour with God than a thousand with the sweetest society on earth or in Heaven. All other joys are but streams; God is the fountain (Robert Murray M'Cheyne).

Day Eighty-Nine

All Things Are Possible

But Jesus looked at them and said to them, "With men this is impossible, but with God all things are possible."
Matthew 19:26, NKJV

God's power is not dependent upon man or some other source. He does not have to muster up an anointing or try to make power flow. He is God and in Him is the greatest of all power and authority. There is nothing that compares to His power and strength.

With a word, He drives out the enemies. With a word, He creates the universe. His power is not diminished when things "aren't going His way." His power is always supreme, always flowing, always working.

"With God all things are possible" because He is the creator of all things and thus can sustain and advance anything He chooses. He bestows His power and great works upon His children. He meets the wicked with power that holds them out of destruction until the appointed time. He preserves His children with His great power.

As God's presence is eternal and immense, so is His power. He holds all power and ability. As God is almighty, He is also all knowing and understanding in the use of His power. He knows what we have need of and utilizes His power with wisdom to work on our behalf. He knows exactly how to sustain the universe and all that is within it. He knows how to execute His sovereign plan and uses His great power to bring it to pass.

God's power is like Himself, self-existent, self-sustained. The mightiest of men cannot add so much as a shadow of increased power to the Omnipotent One. He is Himself the great central source and originator of all power (Charles Spurgeon).

He is able to save to the uttermost (Hebrews 7:25). He is able to help those who are being tempted (Hebrews 2:18). He is able to guard what has been committed to Him (2 Timothy 1:12). He is able to keep you from stumbling (Jude 1:24). He is able to do far more abundantly (Ephesians 3:20). He is able to strengthen you (Romans 16:25).

His power is accessible to you. He is at work for you. His power can save. His power can heal. His power can deliver. If you will place a demand on His anointing by faith, His anointing will bring miracles in your life. All things are possible with God. The salvation of your family is possible. The healing of your body is possible. The deliverance from sin is possible.

Look to Christ today for His power for your life. Look to Christ for His power for the lives of those around you.

Day Ninety
Consider Jesus

Therefore, holy brethren, partakers of the heavenly calling, consider the Apostle and High Priest of our confession, Christ Jesus.
Hebrews 3:1, NKJV

Let us fasten our eyes on the Apostle and the High Priest of our faith, Christ Jesus. He is the Author, the Finisher, and the Perfecter of our faith. We are transformed as we set our gaze upon Christ. Beholding His beauty, we become more like Him.

Consider Christ's deity. In Him is the radiance of the Father. He is the outshining of God's glory. Just as the rays of the sun radiate its light, so Christ is the radiance of the Father. We have seen the glory of the Father in Christ (John 1:14). In Christ's transfiguration, we see the brightness of the Father in Christ (Matthew 17:1-5).

In His radiance, He gives glory to His church. The church is shining with the glory of God (Isaiah 60). Christ is the Word that illuminates our path (Psalm 119:105). He removes all confusion and brings guidance for our journey. He clothes His people with glorious light. And in His beams, there is healing and transformation (Malachi 4:2). Christ has risen over you today with the glory of God in His beams!

Christ Jesus is the exact imprint of the Father. If you have seen Christ, you have seen the Father (John 14:9). He is the infallible nature of God brought to mankind. In Christ we do not have to look through eyes of faith, but in Him, we see the manifestation of God. God desired us to have restored fellowship with Him, so He came into creation as a man that we might behold Him, touch Him, and hear Him. This was no accident It was always the plan. He wanted us to see a tangible representation of His idea of Himself, and so Christ came as the only begotten of the Father (John 1:18).

In Christ's deity, He is upholding all things (Hebrews 1:3). The government of all creation is upon His shoulders (Isaiah 9:6). Nothing is out of His gaze, but everything is laid bare before Him (Hebrews 4:13).

As the Apostle of your faith, He was sent of God to represent God to you. As the High Priest of your faith, He is representing you to God. He has brought the message of redemption, become your sacrifice, carried your punishment, and brought eternal life. Christ is able to redeem, restore, justify, and preserve you as His inheritance.

Consider Jesus today. Turn your attention from worldly lusts and pleasure to find supreme satisfaction in Him. Surrender you gaze to Christ today. He is worthy of your attention, and His radiance will delight your senses, illuminate your heart, transform you into the glory of a child of God, and bring rule and order to your life.

The matchless beauty of Christ will captivate you. Let us fix our eyes on Jesus who, for the joy set before Him, took hold of us!

Spiritual Heritage

It is impossible to create an exhaustive list of every person that has emblazoned a path of significant spiritual heritage in a pursuit of God and revival. Here are some of those that have influenced this writing.

Arnott, John (1940-Present): John and Carol Arnott are best known globally as the pastors that experienced the Toronto Outpouring, which also became known as the "Father's Blessing" in 1994. Pastor, author, husband, father, businessman, Arnott has a rich and blended ministry. He has been welcomed in cities and nations where he has held conferences, services, and special revival meetings.

Bailey, Frank (To Present): Pastor Frank Bailey is the founder and senior pastor of Victory Fellowship (est. 1979) in New Orleans. He and his wife Parris have a passion to see God's glory spread, and this has motivated their life and work. Their ministry is well known for Beyond the Grave, a multi-media evangelistic production launched in 1999, and Feed the Multitudes, an annual free food festival on July 4th. In 1994, the church became a center for revival, which impacted the nations and the Gulf Coast. Their ministry still carries the sound of revival today. Pastor Frank is the author of several books, with two of his books being published by Destiny Image.

Barnes, Albert (1798-1870): Born in Rome, New York, Barnes graduated from Hamilton College in 1820 and from Princeton Theological Seminary in 1823. Barnes was an eloquent preacher known for his expository works, which are said to have had a larger circulation in both Europe and America than any other of their kind. By 1870, more than a million volumes of the well-known *Notes on the New Testament* were issued.

Bartleman, Frank (1871-1936): Bartleman was an author, preacher, missionary that was influenced by the Azusa Street Revival. He wrote many articles for magazines describing the work, and documented much of the revival happenings.

Baxter, Richard (1615-1691): Baxter's industrious nature and talent helped him become a widely learned man. By 1640, he had become a pastor devoted to his flock. He was an English Puritan, poet, hymn-writer, and theologian. He was greatly influenced by John Owen.

Blackaby, Henry T. (To Present): Henry Blackaby is the founder of Blackaby Ministries International and an influential evangelical pastor. He has authored many books and articles. He has pastored both in the United States and Canada. He has served with the International Missions Board and LifeWay Christian Resources. He was president of the Canadian Baptist Theological College for seven years.

Bonar, Andrew (1810-1892): Was a minister of the Free Church of Scotland. He was identified with evangelical and revival movements, alongside of Robert Murray McCheyne. He is the author of several works and endeavored to compile books on McCheyne, Samuel Rutherford and others.

Bonnke, Reinhard (To Present): Reinhard Bonnke is a German Pentecostal evangelist widely known for his missions throughout Africa. He was called to preach in Africa at the age of 10, and he has served in there since 1967. He has authored several books and is considered by many to have lead the way in Pentecostal evangelism.

Brainerd, David (1718-1747): Brainerd is a celebrated missionary to the American Indians. He was born in Haddam, Connecticut and orphaned at 14. During his short life, he experienced many shortcomings. His life became a encouragement to many missionaries including William Carey and Jim Elliot. He found great success in ministry to the Delaware Indians. In November 1746, he became too ill to continue in ministry. He eventually stayed with Jonathan Edwards in Northampton, Massachusetts. In May 1747, he was diagnosed with incurable consumption (tuberculosis). He died at the age of 29. Jonathan Edwards edited and published his diary, which has become known by many as the launch for the modern missionary movement.

Browne, Rodney Howard (To Present): Rodney is a Pentecostal pastor and evangelist from South Africa. He and his wife founded The River at Tampa Bay church in 1996 and together lead Revival Ministries International. In 1989, in upstate New York, revival began to be experienced in his meetings. Eventually, he held a long-term meeting in Lakeland, Florida and then began to hold revival meetings around the world. His ministry is characterized by supernatural signs and wonders with an emphasis on evangelism.

Calvin, John (1509-1564): Calvin was an influential French theologian during the Protestant Reformation. Calvin was influenced by the Augustinian teachings. He authored multiple works and commentaries. Originally trained as a humanist lawyer, he broke from the Roman Catholic Church around 1530. His development of the system of Christian theology later called Calvinism focused particularly on the doctrines of predestination, the absolute sovereignty of God in salvation, and eternal damnation.

Edwards, Jonathan (1703-1758): Born in Connecticut, Edwards caused a turn in American preaching. It is said that, since his day, no one merely possessing an eloquent tongue and skilled mind could make such an impression from the pulpit. Edwards was pastor during the First Great Awakening at his church in Northampton, Massachusetts. He authored many books, and many of his sermons have been published by Yale Press. He entered Yale College in 1716, just under the age of 13. He graduated in 1720 as valedictorian. Edwards along with his friend, George Whitefield, were the most influential men throughout the Thirteen Colonies during this time.

Finney, Charles (1792-1875): Finney was a lawyer by trade, who eventually was converted and Baptized in the Holy Spirit. After his ordination in 1824, he began to evangelize and drew great attention. His message emphasized the deity of Christ, justification by grace through faith, and the power of the Holy Spirit to transform. Finney became one of the first evangelists to popularize the "altar call."

Green, Keith (1953-1982): Green's short-lived Christian life of only twenty-eight years made a massive impact in the music world but also in thousands of lives affected by his revival passion. Converted during the Jesus Movement, he had a great influence with young people, and his *Last Days Ministries Magazine* featured articles from preachers on revival and had a circulation of a quarter of a million. Green died in 1982, in a plane crash with two of his children along with a visiting church planter family.

Henry, Matthew (1662-1714): Henry was a Welsh commentator, known for his six-volume *Exposition of the Old and New Testaments* or *Complete Commentary*. His commentaries provide an exhaustive verse by verse study of the Bible. Henry has authored other works as well. In May 1714, after being stricken with paralysis, he was quoted as saying, "You have been used to take notice of the sayings of dying men; this is mine: That a life spent in the service of God, and communion with Him, is the most pleasant life that anyone can live in this world."

Hill, Steve (1954-2014): Hill is best known as the evangelist who preached in what became known as the Brownsville Revival. The revival began on Father's Day 1995 and continued for five years. In 2000, Hill moved to the Dallas area to continue his traveling ministry. In 2003, he founded Heartland World Ministries Church in Irving, Texas. As a teenager, he was heavily involved with drugs and alcohol. In 1975, he gave his life to Jesus. He was facing 25 years in prison for drug trafficking and was remanded to Teen Challenge. Eventually, he and his wife became missionaries and church planters. In March 2014, Hill died from melanoma.

Joyner, Rick (To Present): Rick Joyner is the pastor of MorningStar Fellowship Church in Fort Mill, South Carolina. Author of numerous books, Joyner is an active promoter of spiritual awakening and revival. He also leads MorningStar

Ministries and Publications, which he cofounded with his wife, Julie, in 1985.

Kendall, R.T. (To Present): Kendall pastored Westminster Chapel in London for 25 years and is the author of more than 50 books. He has a reformation background with Pentecostal influence. He continues to travel and minister and is a regular contributor to Christian publications.

Kilpatrick, John (To Present): Largely known as the Pastor of Brownsville Assembly of God in Pensacola, Florida that experienced the "Brownsville Revival". Currently, Kilpatrick serves as the pastor of Church of His Presence in Daphne, Alabama and travels extensively across the nation spreading the fires of revival.

Kuhlman, Kathryn (1907-1976): Born in Concordia, Missouri and born again at the age of 14 in the Methodist Church, she began preaching at the age of 16, primarily in Baptist Churches. Eventually, she received the Baptism in the Holy Spirit and began holding miracle crusades. In the 1960's and 70's, she had a TV program called *I Believe in Miracles* that was aired nationally. She was well known for significant miracles and her teaching on the Holy Spirit.

Luther, Martin (1483-1546): Luther was a professor of theology and widely known for his influence in the Protestant Reformation. Initially an Augustinian friar, Luther came to reject several teachings and practices of the Roman Catholic Church. He confronted indulgences, salvation by dead works among many others. He nailed his Ninety-Five Theses on the door of All Saints' Church in Wittenberg on October 31, 1517. He is also the author of hymns, commentaries, and the first to translate the Bible into German which made the doctrines of salvation by faith alone accessible to the people.

Maclaren, Alexander (1826-1910): Alexander was Scottish Bible scholar who served as president of the Baptist Union of Great Britain and the Baptist World Congress in London. He is considered an expert expositor of the 19th century.

McPherson, Aimee Semple (1890-1944): "Sister Aimee" was a Canadian-American Los Angeles-based evangelist and media celebrity. She founded the Foursquare Church. She is a noted pioneer in the use of modern media, as she used radio in her ministry. She ministered at Angelus Temple. She was known for her healing ministry and unique preaching style. She was a product of the Azusa Street Revival.

Moody, D.L. (1837-1899): Dwight Lyman Moody, known as D.L. Moody was an American evangelist and publisher who founded Moody Church, Northfield School and Mount Hermon School, the Moody Bible Institute and Moody Publishers. He was raised in the Unitarian Church. In 1855, he was converted at the Congregational Church of Mount Vernon. Moody's ministry is one of international recognition and had a great influence on evangelistic ministry.

Nee, Watchman (1903-1972): Watchman was a church leader and teacher in China. His church meetings were considered by some to be the beginning of local churches in China. He trained many Bible students and church workers. Nee was persecuted and imprisoned for his faith and spent the last twenty years of his life in prison. He was the author of several books.

Parker, Rev. Joseph (1830-1902): One of the greatest preachers of the nineteenth century, Parker preached his first sermon at 18 years of age. He became the pastor of City Temple in London, where he preached for 33 years. His was the second largest congregation in that city, after that of Charles Spurgeon's Metropolitan Tabernacle. One of his best-known works is the *The People's Bible*.

Pratney, William (To Present): With a background in analytical research chemistry, "Winkie's" conversion and calling to minister to the young led him to a series of studies to find some of the fundamental keys in motive and message that marked off some of the heroes of revival history. He has a passion to see each new generation have an ongoing and transforming encounter with God.

Price, Dr. Charles (1887-1947): A Baptist preacher that was baptized in the Holy Spirit at an Aimee Semple McPherson meeting in 1921, He had a significant healing ministry and became one of the most well-known Pentecostal evangelists of the twentieth century. He went from skeptic to believer after he witnessed the healing power of God.

Ravenhill, Leonard (1907-1994): Ravenhill was one of the greatest preachers of revival in the twentieth century. He was born in England, educated at Cliff College, and sat under the ministry of Samuel Chadwick. He was the author of multiple books. His most notable book is *Why Revival Tarries* which has sold over a million copies world-wide.

Seymour, William J. (1870-1922): Well known as the leader of the Azusa Street Revival, he was a one-eyed, black man during a time of racial divide, from St. Mary's Parish in Louisiana. He was the son of slaves. The emphasis of his ministry was the Baptism in the Holy Spirit. There is a wealth of knowledge on Azusa Street and the ministry of William Seymour that is worth personal study.

Simpson, A.B. (1843-1919): Albert Benjamin "A.B." Simpson was a Canadian preacher, founder of the Christian and Missionary Alliance (CMA), and an evangelical Protestant. He had an emphasis on global evangelism. During the early twentieth century, Simpson became closely involved with the growing Pentecostal movement. Simpson also composed lyrics for over 120 hymns.

Saint Augustine (354-430): St. Augustine of Hippo is considered to be one of the early church fathers. He was an Christian theologian and philosopher. Among his most important works are *City of God* and *Confessions*. He was converted in 387. Many Protestants consider Augustine to be a theological father of the Protestant Reformation because of his teachings on salvation and divine grace.

Spurgeon, Charles (1834-1892): He was England's best-known preacher for most of the second half of the nineteenth century. Called the "Prince of Preachers," Spurgeon's evangelistic and pastoral ministry yearly touched hundreds of thousands of people—if not millions in his writings. In 1854, just four years after his conversion, Spurgeon, then only twenty years old, became the pastor of London's famed New Park Street Church. He is the author of volumes of sermons, commentary, and devotional studies.

Taylor, James Hudson (1832-1905): Taylor was a missionary to China. Spurgeon considered Taylor to have a wonderful work of faith, one of the most remarkable in modern times. He recruited over 800 missionaries who began 125 schools. Their work directly resulted in 18,000 Christian conversions as well as the establishment of more than 3,000 stations of work with more than 500 helpers in all 18 provinces and led over 100,000 Chinese to Christ.

Tenney, Tommy (To Present): Tommy saw an incredible visitation in a Houston church that affected his ministry and meetings all over the world. Over three million copies of Tenney's books have been sold. His book on Queen Esther, *Hadassah* was made into a movie.

Tozer, A.W. (1897-1963): Tozer was an American Protestant pastor, author, magazine editor, Bible conference speaker, and spiritual mentor. Two of his works are considered Christian classics: *The Pursuit of God* and *The Knowledge of the Holy*. For his work, he received two honorary doctorates. He would sometimes co-minister with his friend Leonard Ravenhill. Tozer, in his public and his personal life called for revival in the church.

Truscott, Graham (To Present): The Truscotts are missionary pastors to hundreds of churches and ministers around the world. Their travels for Christ have taken them to over 60 nations. Graham is known as a missionary statesman, Bible teacher, church planter, musician, author, and trainer of men and women for ministry. He is the author of numerous articles and nine published books.

Wigglesworth, Smith (1859-1947): Wigglesworth was a humble and almost illiterate plumber, who was taught to read his Bible by the Holy Spirit. Wigglesworth accurately memorized the entire New Testament,daily prayed over it in tongues, and meditated at least four hours a day. He claimed this was the secret to how God used him in winning some two million souls to Christ.

Williams, J. Rodman (1918-2008): Williams is considered to be the father of modern Renewal Theology and was a charismatic theologian. He was a professor at Regent University. With a Presbyterian background, he became involved in the Charismatic Presbyterian Communion. His important works include a three-volume systematic theology titled *Renewal Theology*, the first systematic theology written from a Pentecostal perspective.

Woodworth-Etter, Maria (1844-1924): She began an influential ministry of healing in 1876, later associated with the Methodist Holiness Church. She remained active in revival meetings until the 1920s. She battled prejudice over women in ministry. Her ministry was characterized by significant miracles and salvation of the lost.

Yonggi Cho, David (To Present): Cho is a Korean Christian minister, senior pastor and founder of the Yoido Full Gospel Church (Assemblies of God), the world's largest church with a claimed membership of over 800,000. Raised Buddhist, he was converted to Christianity at age 17, after a girl visited him daily telling him about Jesus. Cho has an international ministry, has authored books and articles, and is considered to be a leading authority on cell or small group ministry.

Zinzendorf, Count Nicolaus Ludwig (1700-1760): The Order of the Mustard Seed came out of a revival among four friends of the persecuted United Brethren.. They launched one hundred 24/7 prayer meetings, and one of the most powerful revival-based mission movements. John Jus who founded United Brethren, was preaching justification by faith and authority of Scripture a hundred years before Luther and was burned at the stake in 1415. Refugees from this persecution made a home under the care of Count Zinzendorf. Their motto became, "To win for the Lamb the reward of His suffering." The Moravians' ministry that was the result, touched multitudes, including John Wesley.

CPSIA information can be obtained
at www.ICGtesting.com
Printed in the USA
LVHW051239130920
665849LV00003B/5